The Art of the Picnic

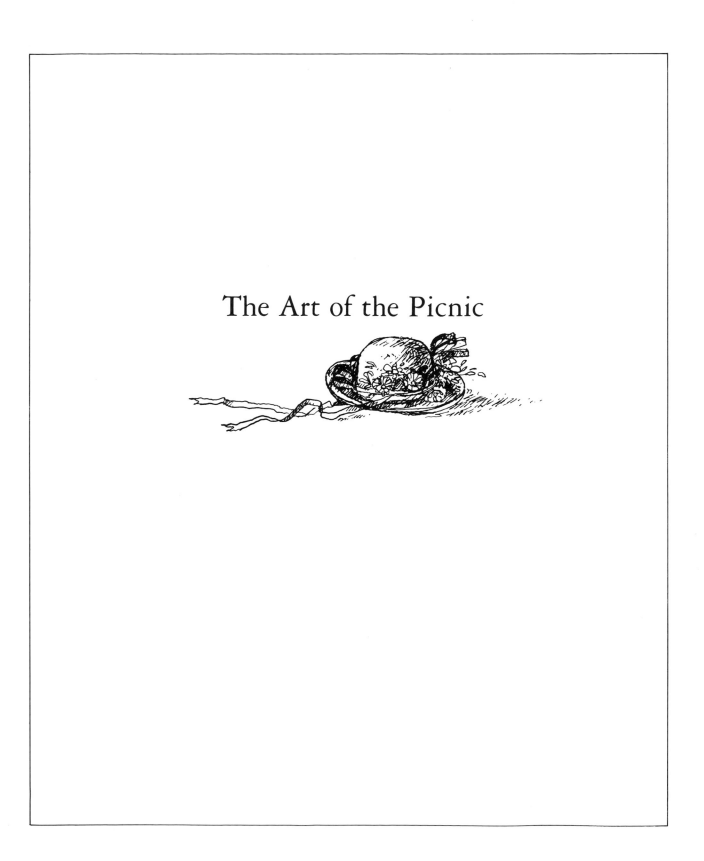

The Art of the Picnic

An anthology of theme picnics with
over a hundred tempting recipes

Pictures by Pamela Kay

Recipes by Susie Ward

CASSELL

London

for Anthony John,
Sydney John & Christopher Robin
all great lovers
of food

First published 1988 by Cassell Publishers Ltd,
Artillery House, Artillery Row, London SW1P 1RT

An Albion Book

Conceived, designed and produced by The Albion Press Ltd,
P.O. Box 52, Princes Risborough, Aylesbury, Bucks HP17 9PR

Designer: Andrew Shoolbred
Editor: Josephine Christian

British Library Cataloguing In Publication Data
Ward, Susan, 1947 –
    The art of the picnic
    1.Food: Dishes for picnics – Recipes
    I.Title II. Kay, Pamela
    ISBN 0 304 321 893

Typesetting and origination by York House, London
Printed and bound in Italy by New Interlitho

The Albion Press would like to thank the copyright holders for permission to
quote from copyright works, and apologize for any inadvertent breach of
copyright.

For help in various ways, the Albion Press would like to thank:
Chris Beetles and the staff of Chris Beetles Ltd, Peter & Sylvia Bradford,
John Coulson, Margaret Craig, Jane Havell, Tristram Holland, Mary
Hutchinson, Robyn Marsack, Christopher Martyn, Anne Neuburg, Nick Trent,
Mary & Michael Whitby.

Contents

Picnic Etiquette

*There is much more to a successful picnic than
remembering to pack the corkscrew.*

If my daughter were to ask my advice about the contribution she should make
to a picnic, I should say to her: 'If you bring the desserts, the guests will be
satisfied. If you choose the cheeses, they will repay you with gratitude.' But my
daughter doesn't ask my advice. One day, when we were both invited to the
same improvised meal, I saw that she had brought not only the desserts but
the cheese as well. And I blushed with pride.

COLETTE *Paysages et Portraits* 1958

A picnic should be held among green things. Green turf is absolutely an
essential. There should be trees, broken ground, small paths, thickets, and
hidden recesses. There should, if possible, be rocks, old timber, moss, and
brambles. There should certainly be hills and dales, – on a small scale; and
above all, there should be running water.

ANTHONY TROLLOPE *Can You Forgive Her?* 1865

Picnic Etiquette

According to the Concise Oxford Dictionary, a picnic is 'a meal taken out of doors'. By this definition, the office worker's sandwich, eaten in a sunny corner of some city square, is as much a picnic as any multi-course extravaganza produced from the interior of a deep wicker basket. But to the connoisseur, a picnic does imply a certain sense of occasion. Before I will honour a meal outdoors with the name of picnic, it has to fulfil three further stipulations. To give the proper pleasure of anticipation, it should be planned ahead, even if the plan is only formed an hour before departure. There should *be* a departure: a picnic ought to involve a journey, if only from the back door to a table under a garden tree. And a picnic should include food that tastes best out in the open air.

I remember a very limited but quite wonderful picnic of tomatoes, boiled eggs, goat's cheese, rough bread and sweetish local red wine, taken every day to a rocky, fir-bordered inlet on a small island in Yugoslavia some twenty years ago. Every day for two weeks it was exactly the same, because that was all there was on that small outcrop in the Adriatic, anyway at prices an impecunious, itinerant student could afford. But somehow it was marvellous, even in repetition – the tomatoes redder and juicier than ever before or since, the cheese sharp and clean, the egg eggy. But the real wonder was the wine. Sipped from a stemmed wine glass in an indoor dining room, it would have been deemed hardly drinkable, even in those innocent days. In the open air, with a sea breeze blowing and a Mediterranean sun overhead, it tasted like nectar.

I have had similar experiences several times since, and, in a rush of romantic *gourmandise*, I have lugged back from holidays abroad wines, cheeses, pâtés and preserved fruits which showed quite another side of their character when served at home. Invariably, they had formed part of an open-air feast, eaten overlooking some picturesque harbour or some green valley dappled with wild flowers. Spirit of place has great power over food.

Picnic fare served on home turf is not usually quite so unpredictable. We have more control over it; we can pick and choose, prepare and cook what we take. But even so, every picnic has its own personality imposed by circumstances. Time, place, weather, as well as people and food, all play their part. And the circumstances of an outdoor meal are particularly susceptible to alteration. It takes a special blend of imagination and organization to get the balance of ingredients just right, yet flexible enough to change – literally – with the winds. As Henry James observed, an ideal picnic should be 'not so good as to fail of an amusing disorder, nor yet so bad as to defeat the proper function of repasts'. That notion of transience and the ephemeral, counterpointed by real, substantial food, is the very essence of the picnic.

Seasonal eating out of doors is tolerated – indeed, positively encouraged – in almost every culture. Indeed, offhand, the only non-enthusiasts that come to mind are the Eskimos, for even the Laplanders have their midsummer reindeer barbecues.

Some societies treat outdoors feasts as celebrations of the local cuisine: witness, in America, the mint julep and burgoo parties of the Kentucky Derby, the Texan chilli cook-offs; and in the Middle East the Saudi picnic, with its *mechoui* of whole roasted sheep and great piles of flat, flaky bread, eaten on patterned carpets spread out on the desert sands.

Elsewhere in the Arab world, in Egypt, the Day of the Dead, which immediately follows the Coptic Easter, is a national holiday set aside for family picnics at the gravesides of relatives. It is not a time for sadness but for reaffirming the bonds of love that death cannot destroy – and how better to do it than over food? To the Japanese the spring flowering of the cherry trees, the blooms of which last only a few days, is the signal for merriment. Workers and their families abandon dull care and sit with *sushi* and *sake* under the lacy white boughs.

Other cultures treat the picnic more casually – no excuses needed. The Germans enjoy a good *Landpartie* – the more the merrier – while the French will take a *déjeuner sur l'herbe* at the pop of a cork.

But, in the end, the past masters of the picnic are the English. For as Georgina Battiscombe points out in her book on *English Picnics,* 'A picnic is the Englishman's grand gesture, his final defiance flung in the face of fate. No climate in the world is less propitious to picnics than the climate of England, yet with a recklessness which is almost sublime the English rush out of doors to eat a meal on every possible and impossible occasion.'

The twenty-six picnics set out in this book have been designed to suit a variety of occasions and non-occasions; in style they range from basic simplicity, through elegance, to grandeur. But they do have certain characteristics in common. All the food is of the kind that tastes particularly good out of doors. Except for the dishes to be cooked at the barbecue, and an occasional warming soup, nothing needs to be served hot (in the open, hot food can become unappetizingly tepid food at quite remarkable speed). Finally, all the portions specified are of a size intended to satisfy appetites sharpened by fresh air.

Now, let the quotations, the recipes and Pamela Kay's evocative paintings inspire you. Pack your basket, gather your family and friends – and depart for your own perfect picnic.

Breakfast on a Train

*As Colonel Layton notes,
a picnic on a train
has its own special flavour.*

She heaved the valise up on to the upper-bunk, heard him move, felt his appraisal. She glanced round . . .

'I'll get the tea. Would you like a cold bacon sandwich?'

'Cold bacon?'

'Cold fried bacon. I got some last night in Ranpur from the station restaurant.'

'Did you, now!'

She laughed and opened the hamper which he had lifted on to the seat in readiness for breakfast. She loved train journeys. In England as a child she had been disappointed to find how quickly they were over. In an Indian train one could put down roots, stake out claims, enjoy transitory possession for a day or so of a few cubic feet of carriage which even a change of trains did not seem to interrupt.

The hamper belonged to Aunt Fenny and was zinc-lined, with compartments for flasks, cups, knives, spoons, forks and food. The cold fried rashers for sandwiches were in greaseproof paper.

'It's a surprise breakfast. Have a hard-boiled egg first?'

'Hard-boiled eggs too. Well done. No, I'll have a sandwich first.'

When she was a child and before the years of exile at school in England they had trekked on ponies through the Pankot hills, making camp at tea-time, striking camp at dawn; rather, the servants had made camp ahead of them and done all the striking. What's for breakfast? her father used to say. Hard-boiled eggs and cold bacon sandwiches. With mugs of hot sweet tea . . . .

He waited until she made one for herself and then, looking at each other like old conspirators, they bit in, holding their hands up to catch crumbs.

'They taste better on a train,' he said, after swallowing. 'Something to do with the smoke and soot.'

PAUL SCOTT *A Division of the Spoils*, volume 4 of *The Raj Quartet,* 1975

Breakfast on a Train

*This breakfast makes an ample repast, conveniently
packaged for the traveller.*

Giant Carrot-Bran Muffins with Bacon

These muffins stuffed with bacon are different, and
delicious. But if you haven't the time or the inclination
to make them for your picnic, good old-fashioned bacon
sandwiches will do very nicely.

Makes 6 sandwiches

350 g (12 oz) plain white flour	*1 teaspoon ground cinnamon*
170 g (6 oz) wholemeal flour	*½ teaspoon ground nutmeg*
175 g (6 oz) bran cereal flakes	*¾ teaspoon salt*
6 tablespoons brown sugar	*225 g (8 oz) carrots, grated*
2½ teaspoons baking powder	*200 ml (7 fl oz) milk*
	1 large egg
½ teaspoon bicarbonate of soda	*50 g (2 oz) butter, melted*
	Butter, softened
	12 bacon rashers, grilled, rinds removed

Have ready a muffin tin with 12 × 7 cm (2¾ in)
diameter cups, or 6 ramekins of the same diameter.
Grease the tin or ramekins well. Preheat the oven to
200°C/400°F/gas mark 6 if you are using a tin, 190°C/
375°F/gas mark 5 if you are using ramekins.

Mix together all the dry ingredients and stir in the
grated carrots. In another bowl, combine the milk, the
egg and the melted butter, and beat the mixture till it is
frothy. Make a well in the centre of the flour mixture,
pour in the liquid and mix lightly. The batter will be
quite lumpy – don't worry, that's how it's meant to be.

Spoon the mixture into the muffin cups or ramekins: if
you are using a muffin tin, fill alternate cups; set

ramekins about 5 cm (2 in) apart on a baking tray. The
cups will be very full.

Bake the muffins for 25 to 30 minutes, till they are
puffed and golden. Remove them from the oven and let
them cool slightly before lifting them from their tin or
ramekins. Cool for a little longer, then split them,
spread them with butter, and fold two bacon rashers
into each one. Wrap them in plastic film to transport on
the train.

An English Loaf

Makes 1 large loaf

675 g (1½ lb) strong white flour
or 575 g (1¼ lb) white flour and 100 g (4 oz) wholemeal flour

15 g (½ oz) fresh yeast*
450 ml (¾ pint) warm water
20 g (¾ oz) sea salt

Cream the yeast with a little of the water and dissolve the salt in the rest of the water. Put the flour in a large bowl, make a well in the centre and pour in the creamed yeast. Give a quick stir to mix the yeast with the flour, pour in the salty water and stir again to combine all the ingredients. Then knead the dough with your hands (if at any stage it feels too sticky to work, sprinkle over a little more flour). After a few minutes' kneading the dough will feel smooth and springy and come away cleanly from the sides of the bowl. Form the dough into a ball, cover it with a cloth and leave it in a warm place to rise.

In 3 hours or so, the dough will have doubled its volume. Knead it again for 3 or 4 minutes, transfer it to a greased 1 kg (2¼ lb) loaf tin and leave it to rise for a second time. After about 2 hours, when the dough has risen just above the top of the tin, heat the oven to 200°C/400°F/gas mark 6. Put the loaf into the hot oven and bake for 40 minutes. Take it from the tin and, to test whether it is cooked, tap it on the bottom. It should sound hollow. If it has a dull sound, put it back in the oven for 5 minutes, then test again. Leave the loaf to cool on a rack, or lying across the empty tin.

This loaf is perfect for traditional bacon sandwiches, which are ideal for peckish travellers. Fry the bacon until crisp, dry it on kitchen paper and lay it between slices of buttered loaf. Wrap in foil to take on your journey.

*You can use micronized dried yeast instead of the fresh yeast. It usually comes in sachets, each containing enough yeast for 675 g (1½ lb) flour. Mix the yeast with the dry flour, then blend in the salt and water.

Scotch Eggs

Makes 6

6 hard-boiled eggs, shelled
Flour
Salt and pepper
350 g (12 oz) sausage meat
½ teaspoon crumbled dried sage

½ teaspoon crumbled dried thyme
2 lightly beaten eggs
75 g (3 oz) breadcrumbs, toasted
Oil for deep frying

Dip each of the eggs in some flour, seasoned with salt and pepper. In a bowl, work the sausage meat, sage and thyme together. Take the meat mixture out of the bowl and divide it into 6 portions. Flatten each into a patty, put an egg in the centre, and shape the meat around it.

Dip each Scotch egg in the beaten egg, and then in the breadcrumbs. Deep fry them, two at a time, for about 5 minutes, then allow them to cool. Transport them packed in a plastic box, and take plenty of English mustard to serve with them.

A Loaf of Bread

*Though the Bible tells us 'Man shall not live by bread alone',
it also counsels 'Eat thy bread with joy, and
drink thy wine with a merry heart'.*

Then Jesus called his disciples unto him, and said, I have compassion on the multitude, because they continue with me now three days, and have nothing to eat: and I will not send them away fasting, lest they faint in the way.

And his disciples say unto him, Whence should we have so much bread in the wilderness, as to fill so great a multitude?

And Jesus saith unto them, How may loaves have ye? And they said, Seven and a few little fishes.

And he commanded the multitude to sit down on the ground.

And he took the seven loaves and the fishes, and gave thanks, and brake them, and gave to his disciples, and the disciples to the multitude.

And they did all eat, and were filled: and they took up of the broken meat that was left seven baskets full.

And they that did eat were four thousand men, beside women and children.

MATTHEW 15, 32–38

Here with a Loaf of Bread beneath the Bough,
A Flask of Wine, a Book of Verse – and Thou
Beside me singing in the Wilderness –
And Wilderness is Paradise enow.

EDWARD FITZGERALD *The Rubáiyát of Omar Khayyám* 1859

A Loaf of Bread

Bread still provides the basis for most outdoor eating. Here is a picnic of loaves and fishes, with a dessert of pomegranates for an exotic Eastern touch.

Marinated Sardines

Serves 6

12 small to medium sardines	*1 teaspoon finely chopped fresh oregano*
1 bottle of dry white wine	*or ½ teaspoon crumbled dried oregano*
2 tablespoons white wine vinegar	*1 teaspoon salt*
1 onion, thinly sliced	*10 black peppercorns*
1 leek, thinly sliced	*2 lemons, strained juice*
1 carrot, cut into julienne strips	*A few sprigs of fresh parsley, preferably flat*
1 bay leaf	

Begin two days before you wish to serve the fish. Clean and gut the sardines, but leave them whole. Place them in a single snug layer in a flameproof baking dish.

Pour the wine and the vinegar into a saucepan (not aluminium) and add the sliced vegetables, bay leaf, oregano, salt and peppercorns. Bring the marinade to the boil, then leave it to simmer gently for about half an hour. Take it off the heat and allow it to cool.

Pour the marinade, with all its ingredients, over the fish. Put the dish, uncovered, on the heat, and bring the liquid to the boil, then take the dish from the heat and cover it. When it has cooled, transfer it to the fridge and leave overnight.

Strain the marinade off the fish and boil it briskly over a high heat till it is reduced to 300 ml (½ pint). Add the lemon juice and pour the marinade over the fish again. Allow to cool, then cover and chill for 24 hours.

Pack the sardines, interspersed with blades of parsley, into a large plastic box. Pour their marinade over them, cover and transport to the picnic.

Pan Bagnat

Serves 4 to 6

1 long French baguette or round country loaf	*1 275 g (10 oz) bottle of marinated artichoke hearts, drained*
2 tablespoons olive oil	*8 anchovy fillets, rinsed and dried*
1 clove of garlic, crushed	
1 medium onion, very thinly sliced into rounds	*12 black olives, sliced*
225 g (8 oz) tomatoes, peeled and thinly sliced	*5 basil leaves, torn into pieces*
2 green peppers, grilled, peeled and thinly sliced	*Salt and pepper*

Cut the loaf in half horizontally. Dribble and spread the olive oil over both cut surfaces and rub the crushed garlic into them. Lay the onion slices over one of the surfaces. Layer the sliced tomatoes and peppers over the onion. Tear the artichoke hearts into pieces and lay them on top, followed by the anchovy fillets, olive slices and basil leaves. Season the sandwich according to taste. Lay the other half of the loaf on top.

Wrap the entire loaf securely in foil. Place it on a baking tray, put a board on top and a heavy weight on that. Keep in a cool place for at least 3 to 4 hours, preferably overnight.

To transport, wrap the foiled loaf in plastic film or put it in a plastic bag (in case of leakage). Serve cut into thick slices.

Picadillo in Pitta

Makes 6 to 8

2 tablespoons olive oil
900 g (2 lb) minced beef
100 g (4 oz) chopped onions
1 clove of garlic, finely chopped
4 canned jalapeño chillies, drained and chopped
3 or 4 tomatoes, peeled, seeded and roughly chopped
2 tart apples, peeled, cored and roughly chopped

8 black olives, chopped
8 green olives, chopped
50 g (2 oz) raisins or sultanas
Pinch of ground cinnamon
Pinch of ground cloves
¾ teaspoon salt
Pepper to taste
50 g (2 oz) blanched and slivered almonds
6 large or 8 medium pitta breads

Pour the olive oil into a frying pan and heat until a light haze forms on it. Add the meat, stirring it constantly with a wooden fork to break it up into pieces that are as small as possible. When the beef is browned, stir in the onion and the garlic. Cook for about 5 minutes, until the onions are lightly coloured but not brown. Add the chillies, tomatoes, apples, olives, raisins, spices and seasonings, cover, and simmer over a low heat, stirring occasionally, for about 20 minutes.

In the meantime, spread the almond slivers out on a baking tray and toast them under a hot grill for about 3 or 4 minutes, until they are golden. Watch them carefully, to make sure they don't burn. When the picadillo has finished cooking, stir in the almonds. Allow to cool slightly before using.

Fill the pitta pockets with the picadillo and wrap each 'sandwich' in plastic film. Serve with a bowl of yogurt to use as dressing.

Fennel and Orange Salad

Serves 6

4 large oranges
2 tablespoons sunflower oil
2 teaspoons white wine vinegar
1 teaspoon finely chopped fresh rosemary
1 teaspoon mild prepared mustard

4 tablespoons quark or skimmed milk soft cheese
3 tablespoons blanched and slivered almonds
2 large heads fennel, trimmed
Round lettuce leaves

Grate the rind from one of the oranges to give ¼ teaspoon fine zest. Squeeze the juice from one of the oranges and measure off ⅓ cup juice. Peel the remaining oranges, carefully removing the white pith. Slice the fruit across into thin circles.

In a small bowl, mix together the sunflower oil, vinegar, rosemary, mustard, orange rind and juice. Carefully beat in the quark, until it is thoroughly amalgamated with the dressing.

Spread the slivered almonds on a baking tray and toast them under a hot grill for 3 or 4 minutes, until they are just golden.

Remove any leaves from the fennel, and reserve them. Trim off the long stalks and any bruised bits. Cut the heads into quarters, then thinly slice crossways. In a large bowl, toss the fennel in the dressing; cover and chill in the fridge for about 1 hour.

Before leaving for the picnic, line a container with the lettuce leaves. Turn the orange slices into the bowl with the fennel and toss gently in the dressing. Spoon the salad into the picnic container, in the middle of the lettuce leaves. Sprinkle with the toasted almonds. Cover.

Pomegranates with Orange Flower Water

1 pomegranate per person
Orange flower water

Slice the tops off the pomegranates. Gently scoop out the flesh and seeds, and discard the pithy bits. Mix the seeds with a few drops of orange flower water in a small bowl. Spoon the flavoured seeds back into the shells and pack into a plastic box to take to the picnic.

A River Picnic

The Water Rat, having assured the Mole that
'there is nothing — *absolutely nothing — half so much worth doing as simply*
messing about in boats', issues an invitation.

'Look here! If you've really nothing else on hand this morning, supposing we drop down the river together, and have a long day of it?'

The Mole waggled his toes from sheer happiness, spread his chest with a sigh of full contentment, and leaned back blissfully into the soft cushions. '*What* a day I'm having!' he said. 'Let us start at once!'

'Hold hard a minute, then!' said the Rat. He looped the painter through a ring in his landing-stage, climbed up into his hole above, and after a short interval reappeared staggering under a fat, wicker luncheon-basket.

'Shove that under your feet,' he observed to the Mole, as he passed it down into the boat. Then he untied the painter and took the sculls again.

'What's inside it?' asked the Mole, wriggling with curiosity.

'There's cold chicken inside it', replied the Rat briefly, 'coldtonguecold-hamcoldbeefpickledgherkinssaladfrenchrollscresssandwichespottedmeat-gingerbeerlemonadesodawater —'

'O stop, stop,' cried the Mole in ecstasies: 'This is too much!'

'Do you really think so?' inquired the Rat seriously. 'It's only what I always take on these little excursions; and the other animals are always telling me that I'm a mean beast and cut it *very* fine!'

The Mole never heard a word he was saying. Absorbed in the new life he was entering upon, intoxicated with the sparkle, the ripple, the scents and the sounds and the sunlight, he trailed a paw in the water and dreamed long waking dreams.

KENNETH GRAHAME *The Wind in the Willows* 1908

A River Picnic

Pull the boat over to the bank: out come the tubs of potted meat and jars of ruby peppers and tomatoes – and fizz goes the ginger beer! Cut slices fresh from the loaf, spread them generously with the potted meat and add a dollop or two of chutney to the side of your plate. Soon the question will become academic – are you having potted meat with chutney or chutney with potted meat?

Pepper and Tomato Chutney

Makes 3 or 4 jars

75 ml (2½ fl oz) olive oil
450 g (1 lb) Spanish onions, finely chopped
1 kg (2¼ lb) red peppers, seeded and cut into thin rounds
1 large clove of garlic, finely chopped
900 g (2 lb) tomatoes, peeled

1 teaspoon powdered ginger
1 teaspoon mixed ground cloves, cinnamon and allspice
225 g (8 oz) sultanas
450 g (1 lb) sugar
450 ml (¾ pint) red wine vinegar

Pour the oil into a large saucepan or enamelled casserole (do not use aluminium). Heat until warm, then add the onions, peppers and garlic. Sauté over a low heat for 15 minutes; do not allow any of the vegetables to brown. Add the rest of the ingredients – the sugar little by little, tasting for sweetness, and the vinegar last. Bring to a rolling boil, then lower the heat. Simmer gently for 3 to 4 hours, uncovered, stirring occasionally. The chutney is ready when it is quite thick, but still lumpy.

Just before potting, pour boiling water into the jars to sterilize them. Drain thoroughly. Spoon the chutney into the jars and cover securely. Keep at least 6 months before using.

Potted Meat

Makes 575 g (1 ¼ lb)

450 g (1 lb) cooked chicken, ham or beef
175 g (6 oz) butter, softened
1 tablespoon sherry or dry red wine

Salt and pepper
1 tablespoon French mustard (optional)

Chop the cooked meat very finely and pound it hard and thoroughly. Or, alternatively, chop the meat roughly and grind it with the metal blade of a food processor. Add 100 g (4 oz) of the butter and continue to pound, or process, until the meat has the texture of a fairly coarse paste. Add the sherry (for the ham or chicken) or red wine (for the beef), and the salt and pepper (and if using the beef, the optional mustard). Pound or process until the paste is as smooth as possible.

Pack the paste into a jar. Melt the remaining butter and pour it over the paste to seal. When the butter has set, press a piece of greaseproof paper on top and cover the jar with a lid.

24

Lemon Squares

Makes 12 squares

For the base	For the topping
100 g (4 oz) butter, melted	2 eggs
175 g (6 oz) plain white flour	175 g (6 oz) caster sugar
25 g (1 oz) icing sugar	2 tablespoons plain white flour
	½ teaspoon baking powder
	1 lemon, grated rind and 2 tablespoons juice
	Icing sugar

Grease an 18 × 25 cm (7 × 10 in) baking sheet. Preheat the oven to 180°C/350°F/gas mark 4.

Add the melted butter to the flour and sugar in a large bowl, and stir until thoroughly combined. Use your fingers to spread the mixture out on the baking sheet, until the entire sheet is covered: the mixture should be about 1 cm (½ in) deep. Bake for 15 minutes.

In the meantime, put all the topping ingredients into a large bowl and beat them together until they are well combined. When the base has baked for 15 minutes, remove it from the oven and pour the topping mixture over it. Return to the oven and continue baking for a further 20 minutes. Take it from the oven and while it is still warm cut it into squares. Allow to cool and sprinkle liberally with icing sugar. Pack in a plastic box to take to the picnic.

The Perfect Green Salad

Serves 6

For the salad	For the vinaigrette dressing
½ Batavian endive	1 tablespoon French mustard
½ cos lettuce	2 lemons, strained juice
1 large handful watercress	60 ml (2 fl oz) white wine vinegar
Several sorrel leaves	1 teaspoon brown sugar (optional)
	1 teaspoon salt
	Pepper to taste
	300 ml (½ pint) sunflower oil
	150 ml (¼ pint) olive oil

Wash and dry all the leaves thoroughly. Tear them into small pieces and pack them in a plastic bag. Put the bag in a plastic bowl – or any kind of bowl so long as it is easy to pack and carry.

To make the dressing, put the mustard in a small bowl and whisk in the lemon juice and the wine vinegar, and then the sugar (if desired), salt and pepper. Slowly beat in the sunflower oil, poured in a thin stream, and follow this with the olive oil. When thoroughly emulsified, turn into a bottle to take on the picnic.

To serve, empty the leaves into the bowl and toss with as much dressing as is needed to moisten them: do not overdress.

Ginger Beer

Makes about 9 litres (2 gallons)

900 g (2 lb) sugar	2 lemons, thinly sliced
50 g (2 oz) cream of tartar	9 litres (2 gallons) boiling water
50 g (2 oz) fresh ginger root, well bruised	Fresh yeast
	1 egg white

Put the first four ingredients into a large pan or bucket. Pour over the boiling water and stir thoroughly. When the liquid has cooled to lukewarm, add a small piece of yeast – in summer the size of a hazelnut, in the winter a bit more. Leave to stand for 12 hours. For a foaming head, whisk the egg white in a small bowl, then whisk into the ginger beer. Strain the liquid into screw-top jars and store in a cool place.

A Day in the Country

*For some reason, the most disastrous picnics
are often those remembered with the most relish.
Consider Laurie Lee's experience.*

I remember a sweltering August Sunday. Mother said it would be nice to go out. We would walk a short mile to a nice green spot and boil a kettle under the trees. It sounded simple enough, but we knew better. For mother's picnics were planned on a tribal scale, with huge preparations beforehand. She flew round the kitchen issuing orders and the young men stood appalled at the work. There were sliced cucumbers and pots of paste, radishes, pepper and salt, cakes and buns and macaroons, soup-plates of bread and butter, jam, treacle, jugs of milk, and several fresh-made jellies.

The young men didn't approve of this at all, and muttered it was blooming mad. But with a 'You carry that now, there's a dear boy', each of us carried something. So we set off at last like a frieze of Greeks bearing gifts to some woodland god – Mother, with a tea-cloth over her head, gathering flowers as she went along, the sisters following with cakes and bread, Jack with the kettle, Tony with the salt, myself with a jug of milk; then the scowling youths in their blue serge carrying the jellies in open basins – jellies which rapidly melted in the sun and splashed them with yellow and rose. . . .

We were ordered to scatter and gather sticks and to build a fire for the kettle. The fire smoked glumly and stung our eyes, the young men sat round like martyrs, the milk turned sour, the butter fried on the bread, cake crumbs got stuck to the cucumber, wasps seized the treacle, the kettle wouldn't boil and we ended by drinking the jellies.

As we boys would eat anything, anywhere, none of this bothered us much. But the young courting men sat on their spread silk-handkerchiefs and gazed at the meal in horror. 'No thanks, Mrs Lee. I don't think I could, I've just had me dinner, ta.'

LAURIE LEE *Cider with Rosie* 1959

A Day in the Country

This rather different country picnic might have had more success with the young men! What could be more suitable for a country picnic on a summer's day than a velvety soup of fresh lettuce? The smoked turkey and ham sandwiches are substantial without being heavy, and the traditional fruit cake makes a satisfyingly solid dessert. Sparkling elderflower champagne will set off the meal and enliven the party.

Lovely Lettuce Soup

Serves 6

1 large onion, finely chopped
50 g (2 oz) unsalted butter
900 ml (1½ pints) chicken stock
450 g (1 lb) fresh lettuce leaves, rinsed and dried
3 tablespoons finely chopped fresh dill
125 ml (4 fl oz) double cream
Salt and pepper
Grated nutmeg

Cook the onion in the butter over a gentle heat, till it is softened and just coloured. Pour in the chicken stock, stirring, and bring to the boil; continue to boil for 10 minutes or so, till the liquid is reduced by about a third.

Add the lettuce and the the dill, turn down the heat and simmer, stirring occasionally, for about 15 minutes. Take the soup from the heat, add the cream, the salt and pepper and the nutmeg and purée the soup in a blender or food processor. Return to the saucepan and heat gently to help combine the flavours. If you want to serve the soup hot, pour it straight into a warmed vacuum flask; if you are serving it cold, chill till leaving time, then pour it into a vacuum flask.

Smoked Turkey and Ham Sandwiches on Cottage Cheese Bread

Makes about 20 open sandwiches

225 g (8 oz) wholemeal flour
225 g (8 oz) plain white flour
2 teaspoons baking powder
½ teaspoon bicarbonate of soda
¾ teaspoon salt
60 ml (2 fl oz) oil
60 ml (2 fl oz) honey
175 ml (6 fl oz) milk
1 egg, beaten
225 g (8 oz) cottage cheese
Mayonnaise
225 g (8 oz) smoked turkey, thinly sliced
225 g (8 oz) smoked ham, thinly sliced

Preheat the oven to 190°C/375°F/gas mark 5.

Mix the two types of flour, the baking powder, the bicarbonate of soda and the salt in a large bowl. Pour the oil and honey into a small saucepan and stir over a low heat until blended. Remove from the heat and beat in the milk, the egg and the cottage cheese. Pour this mixture into the dry ingredients, stirring all the time to combine. Pour the batter into a buttered and floured loaf tin. To pop out the air bubbles, drop the tin (carefully!) a couple of times, then press gently on the top of the batter with a palette knife. Smooth the top of the loaf. Cook the loaf for about 50 minutes, until the top is golden. Cool the bread for 15 minutes before removing it from the tin, then transfer it to a wire rack. When quite cool, cut into thinnish slices. Spread one side of each slice of bread with mayonnaise; on half the pieces pile thin slices of smoked turkey, on the rest slices of smoked ham. Cut across each piece diagonally, to give two triangular open sandwiches. Pack the two types of sandwiches in two separate containers.

Picnic Fruit Cake

Makes an 18 cm (7 in) square or a 20 cm (8 in) round cake

100 g (4 oz) butter
175 g (6 oz) granulated
 sugar
175 g (6 oz) sultanas
175 g (6 oz) dried
 apricots, chopped
50 g (2 oz) mixed peel
50 g (2 oz) glacé cherries,
 halved
1 teaspoon mixed spice
125 ml (4 fl oz) sherry
125 ml (4 fl oz) water
225 g (8 oz) plain white
 flour
1 teaspoon bicarbonate of
 soda
Pinch of salt
2 eggs, beaten
Cointreau

Preheat the oven to 180°C/350°F/gas mark 4. Grease an 18 cm (7 in) square tin or a 20 cm (8 in) round tin. Put the butter, sugar, sultanas, apricots, peel, cherries, spice, sherry and water into a large saucepan and boil for 1 minute. Pour into a large bowl and allow to cool. Mix together the flour, bicarbonate of soda and salt in another bowl, then stir in the beaten eggs. Slowly pour in the liquid mixture, stirring often. When the pudding is thoroughly combined, pour it into the greased tin and bake for about 1¼ hours, or till a fine skewer pushed into the cake comes out clean.

Leave the cake to cool for 10 minutes before removing it from the tin and transferring it to a wire rack. Pierce the cake in several places with a skewer, and dribble in a little Cointreau. Allow to cool thoroughly, then pack in an airtight container. This cake will keep for several weeks.

Macaroons

Makes about 30 macaroons

100 g (4 oz) blanched
 almonds
225 g (8 oz) caster sugar
2 drops of vanilla essence
2 egg whites
Icing sugar

Preheat the oven to 180°C/350°F/gas mark 4. Line a baking tray with non-stick baking parchment. Put the almonds into a large mortar or a sturdy bowl, and pound them thoroughly, adding the caster sugar little by little, until they are reduced to a fine-textured paste. (Alternatively, you can whizz the almonds in a food processor.) Stir in the vanilla essence, and, stirring all the time, gradually add the egg whites.

Drop teaspoons of the mixture on the baking sheet, making sure that they are well spaced out. Brush the macaroons with water and sprinkle over the icing sugar. Bake until golden – about 15 minutes. Pack them carefully in a plastic box to take to the picnic.

Elderflower Champagne

Elderflower champagne, made when the lacy blooms of the elder blanket the countryside, is a real summer treat.

Makes about 4.75 litres (8½) pints

About 6 large elderflower
 heads
675 g (1½ lb) sugar
2 tablespoons white wine
 vinegar
2 lemons

Put all of the ingredients except the lemons into a large bowl or bucket. Squeeze and quarter the lemons and add the juice and skins to the other ingredients. Allow to stand for 24 hours, stirring occasionally with a long-handled spoon.

Strain the liquid and pour it into screw-top bottles, leaving about 2.5 cm (1 in) empty at the top of each bottle to allow for expansion. Store in a cool, dark place. It will be ready to drink after a couple of weeks, but will continue to improve for about 2 months, and will keep its sparkle for 3 months or so.

A Mushroom Feast

No mushroom will ever taste quite so good
as the one you have picked yourself,
in the woods or the fields.

In one little roadside dell mushrooms might sometimes be found, small button mushrooms with beaded moisture on their cold milk-white skins. The dell was the farthest point of their walk; after searching the long grass for mushrooms, in season and out of season – for they would not give up hope – they turned back and never reached the second milestone.

FLORA THOMPSON *Lark Rise to Candleford* 1945

Sergei Ivanovitch looked at Varenka as she knelt on the grass, defending a mushroom from the attacks of Grisha, to save it for little Masha.

'Did you find any?' she asked, turning her sweet face towards him with a smile.

'Not a single one,' he answered. They walked a few steps in silence. Varenka, stifled with emotion, suspected what Koznuishef had in mind. Suddenly, though not really in the mood for talking, she replied almost involuntarily, –

'If you have not found any, it is because there are never so many mushrooms in the woods as along the edge.'

He made an effort to recall his recent thoughts on the subject of marriage; but instead of the speech which he had prepared, he asked, –

'What difference is there between a birch mushroom and a white mushroom?'

Varenka's lips trembled as she answered, –

'The only difference is in the cap.' Both of them felt that this was the end of it. The words which might have united them were not spoken, and the violent emotion which stirred them died little by little away.

LEO TOLSTOY *Anna Karenina* 1876

A Mushroom Feast

The full, earthy flavour of mushrooms seems especially appropriate for
an outdoor meal. Mushrooms are brown, there's no disguising it.
Brighten up this picnic with cherry tomatoes to accompany the pâté and
crisp red apples to complement the Stilton salad. Serve a red country
wine to bring out the best in the mushrooms and the colour scheme!

Cucumber-Cumin Sambal

Serves 6

4 large cucumbers, peeled,
halved lengthways,
seeded, and cut into
1 cm (½ in) slices
2 teaspoons salt
150 ml (¼ pint) Greek-
style strained yogurt

2 tablespoons white wine
vinegar
1 clove of garlic, crushed
5 teaspoons cumin seed,
pounded and bruised
60 ml (2 fl oz) olive oil

In a large bowl, toss the cucumber slices with the salt.
Leave to stand for 30 minutes.

Meanwhile, whisk together the yogurt, vinegar, garlic
and 4 teaspoons of the cumin seed in a small bowl. Still
whisking, add the oil in a thin stream; whisk till the
mixture is thoroughly blended.

Drain the cucumber slices thoroughly and squeeze
them dry between paper towels. Stir the slices into the
yogurt mixture. Put the remaining cumin seed on a
baking tray and toast under a hot grill for 5 minutes,
watching carefully to make sure it does not burn. Stir
half of the toasted seed into the salad. Transfer the
sambal to a plastic bowl or box and sprinkle the rest of
the toasted cumin seed over the top.

Mushroom Pâté

Serves 6

225 g (8 oz) large open
mushrooms, chopped
25 g (1 oz) butter
2 cloves of garlic, chopped

225 g (8 oz) cream cheese
Soy sauce
2 tablespoons chopped
parsley

Sauté the chopped mushrooms in the butter for 6 or 7
minutes; add the garlic and cook briefly for another
couple of minutes. If you have a large amount of liquid,
boil somewhat to reduce, but do leave some in the pan.
Remove from the heat, pour into the bowl of a blender
or food processor, and add the cream cheese and soy
sauce to taste (start with 1 teaspoon, then add more if
desired). Finally, spoon in the parsley. Turn on the
blender or processor and reduce the mushroom
mixture to a smoothish paste. Scrape into a terrine or
large ramekin and chill till set. Cover with plastic film to
transport, and serve with a rough granary bread.

Sausage and Mushroom Wild Rice Pilaff

Serves 6

100 g (4 oz) wild rice
50 g (2 oz) butter
225 g (8 oz) brown rice
1 large onion, sliced
100 g (4 oz) mushrooms,
    chopped
1 can of beef consommé
900 ml (1½ pints) water
5 sprigs of fresh
    marjoram, chopped
Salt

5 Polish- or Italian-style
    sweet sausages
100 g (4 oz) feta cheese,
    cubed
75 g (3 oz) pitted olives,
    chopped
A large handful of mint,
    finely chopped
About 600 ml (1 pint)
    vinaigrette dressing (see
    page 25)

Rinse and drain the wild rice. Meanwhile, in a large frying pan, melt the butter and sauté the brown rice and the onion for about 10 minutes over a low heat. Add the mushrooms and sauté for a further 2 minutes. Pour in the beef consommé, the water, the wild rice and the marjoram; add salt to taste. Bring to the boil, then reduce the heat, cover and simmer for 50 to 60 minutes, until all the rice is tender and the liquid absorbed. Pour the rice into a bowl and allow to cool.

Meanwhile, pre-heat the oven to 200°C/400°F/gas mark 6. Slash the curved side of each sausage a few times. Cook the sausages in the oven for 20 to 30 minutes, or till they are browned and sizzling. Allow to cool.

Chop the sausages into bite-sized pieces and add them to the rice in the bowl. Stir in the cheese, olives and mint. Pour over as much vinaigrette dressing as liked, cover the bowl with plastic film, and chill. Take the pilaff to the picnic in its bowl, or transfer it to a plastic box.

Stilton Salad

Serves 6 to 8

275 g (10 oz) Stilton,
    cubed
225 g (8 oz) shelled
    walnuts, halved or
    chopped
1 bunch of celery,
    trimmed and chopped

For the dressing
2 tablespoons Dijon
    mustard
4 tablespoons red wine
    vinegar
8 tablespoons walnut oil
Salt and pepper

In a large bowl, combine all of the salad ingredients. In a small bowl, beat the mustard with the wine vinegar. Beating all the time, pour in the walnut oil in a thin stream. Season to taste with salt and pepper. Pour the dressing over the salad, and spoon it into a plastic bowl or box. Chill until you are ready to leave.

A Picnic Party

The nineteenth-century clergyman Francis Kilvert recorded a neighbourly picnic party, in a passage which now evokes the pleasures of a vanished era.

The company and provisions were packed into the four carriages and the procession set out through the narrow lanes. At the foot of the Castle Hill we got out and every one carried something up the steep slippery brown bare grass slopes.

A fire was to be lighted to boil potatoes which had been brought with us. [After a succession of accidents with the fire and the potatoes] at length the pot was settled upright on the embers. Twenty minutes passed, during which the gentlemen stood round the fire staring at the pot, while the ladies got flowery wreaths and green and wild roses to adorn the dishes and table cloth spread under an oak tree and covered with provisions. Then the pot hook was adjusted, the pot heaved and swung off the fire, a fork plunged into the potatoes and they were triumphantly pronounced to be done to a turn. Then there was a dispute how they should be treated. 'Pour away the water,' said one. 'Steam the potatoes', 'Pour them out on the ground', 'Hand them round in the pot','Fish them out with a fork'. Eventually the potatoes were handed round the table cloth, every one being most assiduous and urgent in recommending and passing them to his neighbour. Then there was plenty of meat and drink, the usual things, cold chicken, ham and tongue, pies of different sorts, salads, jam and gooseberry tarts, bread and cheese. Cup of various kinds went round, claret and hock, champagne, cider and sherry, and people sprawled about in all attitudes and made a great noise. After luncheon the gentlemen entrenched themselves upon a fragment of the Castle wall to smoke and talk local news and politics and the ladies wandered away by themselves.

FRANCIS KILVERT *Diary* 21.6.1870

A Picnic Party

*This is not a picnic for refined appreciation – its flavours are assertive
and vibrant. The roll of beef which is its centrepiece is both festive and
filling. Its multilayered stuffing, containing cheese, eggs, vegetables
and yet more meat, will cater to hearty appetites stimulated by games
and fresh air.*

Stuffed Beef Roll

Serves 6 hungry people

1.5 kg (3 lb) rump steak, trimmed of excess fat, in one piece	*Salt and pepper*
	75 g (3 oz) Emmenthal cheese, cut in 4 slices
350 g (12 oz) spinach, trimmed and washed	*4 slices ham*
450 g (1 lb) minced beef	*2 tablespoons olive oil*
5 eggs, 4 hard-boiled and shelled, 1 lightly beaten	*1 carrot, chopped*
	2 celery stalks, with leaves, chopped
2 tablespoons breadcrumbs	*1 onion, chopped*
	A glass of red wine
1 clove of garlic, crushed	*2 teaspoons tomato purée*

Place the steak between 2 pieces of greaseproof paper
and pound it till it is as flat and thin as you can get it. In
a saucepan, wilt the spinach in the water clinging to its
leaves from washing. Remove it from the heat and allow
it to cool a little. Mix the minced beef, the beaten egg,
the breadcrumbs and the garlic and season with salt and
pepper. Work the mixture with your hands till the
ingredients are thoroughly combined.

Remove the paper from the steak. Distribute the spinach
evenly over the steak to within 2.5 cm (1 in) of the
edges. On top of this, overlap the slices of cheese, and
then the slices of ham. Place the four hard-boiled eggs
in a line down the centre, trimming the ends of the eggs
so that they fit together more snugly. Roll the steak into
a tight cylinder around the eggs. Using heavy string, tie
the roll lengthways, tucking the ends in. Then tie the
meat crossways in several places.

Preheat the oven to 180°C/350°F/gas mark 4. Heat the oil
in a heavy casserole. Add the meat roll and brown it all
over. Lift out the meat and sauté the carrot, the celery
and the onion for a few minutes. Then return the meat
to the casserole, resting it on the vegetables. Pour over
the red wine. When it has cooked a little, stir in the
tomato purée and a glass of water. Cover the casserole
and put it in the oven. Cook for 1¾ hours.

When you take the casserole from the oven, allow the
meat to cool in the sauce, spooning it over occasionally.
Chill overnight, then untie the meat and pack it, with its
sauce, in a large plastic box. Serve in slices.

Potato and Green Bean Salad

Serves 6

6 large potatoes in their skins	*Salt and pepper*
225 g (8 oz) green beans	*6 spring onions, roughly chopped*
About 600 ml (1 pint) vinaigrette dressing (see page 25)	

Boil the potatoes in their skins till they are just tender –
do not overcook them. Allow them to cool slightly
before you peel them. Meanwhile, steam the green
beans, or boil them in a little water. Drain. Cut the
potatoes into bite-sized pieces and the green beans into
about 2.5 cm (1 in) lengths. Toss the still-warm
vegetables in the vinaigrette dressing – as much as is
needed – add salt and pepper to taste, and sprinkle over
the spring onion. Toss again lightly and chill. Before you
pack the salad for the picnic toss it again with more
vinaigrette, since it will have absorbed a good deal while
cooling. Take it to the picnic in a covered plastic bowl.

Walnut Bread with Blue Cheese Spread

Makes a large loaf and almost 225 g (½ lb) cheese

For the bread	For the spread
3 tablespoons unsalted butter	*150 g (6 oz) blue cheese*
175 g (6 oz) brown sugar	*4 tablespoons unsalted butter*
475 ml (¾ pint) yogurt and milk, mixed half and half	*Cayenne pepper*
3 tablespoons golden syrup	*Brandy*
225 g (8 oz) wholemeal flour	
100 g (4 oz) plain white flour	
50 g (2 oz) bran	
2 teaspoons bicarbonate of soda	
1 teaspoon salt	
175 g (6 oz) walnuts, finely chopped	

Preheat the oven to 180°C/350°F/gas mark 4. Grease a 1 kg (2¼ lb) loaf tin. Make the bread. Beat the butter and brown sugar together in a bowl. Slowly beat in the yogurt-milk mixture and the golden syrup. In another bowl mix together the two types of flour, the bran, the bicarbonate of soda, the salt and the walnuts. Gradually, beat the mixed dry ingredients into the wet mixture.

Pour the dough into the greased tin, and bake for between 1¼ and 1½ hours, or till the bread begins to pull away from the sides of the tin. Cool in the tin for about 15 minutes, then turn out on a wire rack to finish cooling.

To make the spread, beat the blue cheese (use Stilton or a French blue – avoid the creamier Italian cheeses) with the butter. Add cayenne pepper to taste, and a little brandy. Leave for at least a couple of hours for the flavours to combine and develop.

Before the picnic, slice the walnut loaf into thin slices. Spread a little of the cheese spread on each slice, and pack them into a plastic box.

Cider Cup

Makes about 2 litres (3½ pints)

1.15 litres (2 pints) medium or sweet cider	*1 lemon, strained juice*
125 ml (4 fl oz) medium or sweet sherry	*2 tablespoons sugar*
60 ml (2 fl oz) brandy	*Grated nutmeg*
	A 1 litre (1¾ pint) bottle of soda water or sparkling mineral water

Put the cider, sherry, brandy and lemon juice in a jug and stir in the sugar and grated nutmeg to taste. Pour into plastic screw-top bottles and chill in the fridge till you are ready to leave. Don't forget to take the sparkling water to the picnic as well – and encourage people to top up each glass with a generous splash of water.

Spicy Fresh Lemonade

Serves 6 to 8

10 to 12 lemons (enough to give 250 ml/8 fl oz juice)	*200 ml (7 fl oz) water*
225 g (8 oz) caster sugar	*8 cloves*
	2×5 cm (2 in) sticks of cinnamon

Squeeze the juice from the lemons. Combine the sugar and water in a saucepan and bring to the boil; cook, stirring, until the sugar is dissolved. Drop the cloves and cinnamon into the syrup and continue to cook for a further 5 minutes. Take the syrup off the heat and pour in the lemon juice. Allow to cool completely, then refrigerate.

Just before going to the picnic, mix the syrup with 1.15 litres (2 pints) of iced water. Pour into vacuum flasks.

A Children's Treat

Enid Blyton said that a picnic was 'the nicest way to eat food'.
Many children would agree –
especially if they had Katy's Aunt Izzie to put up the hamper,
and Katy's makeshift bower to eat it in.

When it was done they all cuddled underneath. It was a very small bower – just big enough to hold them, and the baskets, and the kitten. I don't think there would have been room for anybody else, not even another kitten. Katy, who sat in the middle, untied and lifted the lid of the largest basket, while all the rest peeped eagerly to see what was inside.

First came a great many ginger cakes. These were carefully laid on the grass to keep till wanted; buttered biscuit came next – three apiece, with slices of cold lamb laid in between; and last of all were a dozen hard-boiled eggs, and a layer of thick bread and butter sandwiched with corned-beef. Aunt Izzie had put up lunches for Paradise before, you see, and knew pretty well what to expect in the way of appetite.

Oh, how good everything tasted in that bower, with the fresh wind rustling the poplar leaves, sunshine and sweet wood-smells about them, and birds singing overhead! No grown-up dinner party ever had half so much fun. Each mouthful was a pleasure; and when the last crumb had vanished, Katy produced the second basket, and there – oh, delightful surprise!– were seven little pies, – molasses pies, baked in saucers – each with a brown top and crisp, candified edge, which tasted like toffee and lemon-peel, and all sorts of good things mixed up together.

There was a general shout. Even demure Cecy was pleased, and Dory and John kicked their heels on the ground in a tumult of joy. Seven pairs of hands were held out at once toward the basket; seven sets of teeth went to work without a moment's delay. In an incredibly short time every vestige of pie had disappeared, and a blissful stickiness pervaded the party.

SUSAN COOLIDGE *What Katy Did* 1872

A Children's Treat

Sandwiches are usually popular with children, and it's fun to try imaginative combinations – though it's worth checking first that the children like the separate ingredients. The coblets are small treats for small fingers. For dessert, toothachingly sweet molasses tarts are a favourite of American children. The miniature ginger cakes are rather less gooey!

Medley of Children's Sandwiches

Makes 12 sandwiches, 48 quarters

12 slices brown bread	Lemon juice
12 slices white bread	175 g (6 oz) cream cheese
Butter	Apricot jam
2 apples, peeled and cored	150 g (5 oz) can baked
175 g (6 oz) Cheddar	beans
cheese	4 frankfurters, thinly
2 bananas, peeled	sliced

Butter all the bread. Grate the apples into a bowl, then grate the cheese into the same bowl and mix them together. Put a little of this filling on 3 slices of white bread and cover with the buttered side of 3 other white slices. Cut into quarters.

In another bowl, mash the bananas with a little lemon juice. Spread on 3 of the buttered brown slices and cover with the buttered side of 3 other brown slices. Cut into quarters.

Spread the cream cheese on the buttered side of 3 brown slices; spread the apricot jam on the buttered side of 3 other slices. Sandwich together and cut into quarters.

Drain the baked beans as thoroughly as possible in a small sieve. Then mash with a fork or in a food processor or blender. Spread on 3 buttered white slices and layer the frankfurter slices on top. Cover with the other 3 buttered white slices. Cut into quarters. Pack the quarter-sandwiches into plastic boxes.

Corn Coblets

Enough for 6 to 8 children

6 medium ears of corn, stripped of leaves and husks	2½ tablespoons sugar
	50 g (2 oz) red pimento, finely chopped
175 ml (6 fl oz) white wine vinegar	1 teaspoon mustard seed
1 small onion, finely chopped	1 teaspoon crushed chillies
	½ teaspoon salt

Cut each cob across into 2 cm (¾ in) rounds, using a hammer if necessary to help drive the knife through the cob. In a large pan bring about 4.5 litres (1 gallon) of water to the boil, add the corn coblets, and cook for 3 minutes. Drain the coblets and put them in a large baking dish in as near a single layer as possible.

Pour the vinegar into the large saucepan used to cook the corn. Add the onion, sugar, pimento, spices and salt, and cook, stirring, till the sugar dissolves. Bring to the boil. Pour the sweet-and-sour liquid over the corn and allow to cool, spooning the marinade over the coblets frequently. Chill, covered, for about 6 hours.

Transfer the coblets and their juices to a plastic bowl or box with a secure lid. The children can serve themselves with their fingers.

Minature Gingerbread Cakes

Makes about 20 little cakes

*100 g (4 oz) plain white
    flour*
*½ teaspoon baking
    powder*
*¼ teaspoon bicarbonate
    of soda*
1 teaspoon ground ginger
¼ teaspoon salt
*100 g (4 oz) butter,
    softened*

*100 g (4 oz) light brown
    sugar*
*60 ml (2 fl oz) golden
    syrup*
*60 ml (2 fl oz) low-fat
    yogurt*
1 large egg, beaten
4 teaspoons water
175 g (6 oz) icing sugar

Preheat the oven to 180°C/350°F/gas mark 4. Have ready a muffin tin or a bun tin with deep cups. Mix the flour, baking powder, bicarbonate of soda, ginger and salt together in a large bowl. In another bowl beat the butter and brown sugar with an electric mixer until the mixture is fluffy. Spoon in the golden syrup, the yogurt, the egg and 2 teaspoons of the water and beat until combined (although the mixture will look somewhat curdled and separated). Pour into the flour mixture slowly, stirring. Spoon the mixture into the cups of the tin, filling them about two-thirds full. Bake for about 15 minutes, until a fine skewer comes out clean. Allow to cool slightly, then turn out on a wire rack.

In a small bowl stir together the icing sugar and the remaining 2 teaspoons of water to a smooth white mixture of dropping consistency. Drizzle a little over each little cake and allow it to set. Take the cakes to the picnic in a plastic box. Any that are left over will keep for some time in an airtight container.

Molasses Tarts

Makes 12 small tarts

For the pastry
*200 g (7 oz) plain white
    flour*
1 teaspoon salt
*125 g (4½ oz) margarine
    or half margarine and
    half lard*
About 3 tablespoons water

For the filling
125 g (4½ oz) plain flour
100 g (4 oz) brown sugar
Pinch of salt
½ teaspoon cinnamon
*Large pinch of ground
    ginger*
Large pinch of nutmeg
*50 g (2 oz) butter,
    softened*
*1 teaspoon bicarbonate of
    soda*
6 tablespoons molasses
*6 tablespoons boiling
    water*

Have ready 12 tartlet tins.

Make the pastry first. In a bowl, sift the flour and salt together. Cut in the fat and continue cutting and blending till the mixture looks like breadcrumbs. Sprinkle the water over (use just enough to enable the ingredients to cohere), mix it in with the knife or a fork, and then use your hands to shape it swiftly into a ball. Chill in the fridge for at least 1 hour, or in the freezer for 20 minutes.

Roll out the pastry and cut out 12 circles to line the tins. Put the lined tins into the fridge to chill till you are ready for them.

Preheat the oven to 190°C/375°F/gas mark 5.

Combine the flour, brown sugar, salt and spices, and add the butter in small pieces. Work with the fingers till the mixture resembles breadcrumbs. Reserve.

In another bowl, stir the bicarbonate of soda and the molasses into the boiling water. Add two-thirds of the crumb mixture and combine thoroughly. Pour the filling into the 12 tartlet tins. Sprinkle the remaining crumb mixture over the tops. Bake for about 35 to 40 minutes, until the crust and topping are golden. Cool. Take them to the picnic in a plastic box.

Victorian Abundance

Today's picnickers may need to scale down
Mrs Beeton's lavish
'Bill of Fare for Forty Persons'

A joint of cold roast beef, a joint of cold boiled beef, 2 ribs of lamb, 2 shoulders of lamb, 4 roast fowls, 2 roast ducks, 1 ham, 1 tongue, 2 veal-and-ham pies, 2 pigeon pies, 6 medium-sized lobsters, 1 piece of collared calf's head, 18 lettuces, 6 baskets of salad, 6 cucumbers.

Stewed fruit well sweetened, and put into glass bottles well corked; 3 or 4 dozen plain pastry biscuits to eat with the stewed fruit, 2 dozen fruit turnovers, 4 dozen cheesecakes, 2 cold cabinet puddings in moulds, 2 blancmanges in moulds, a few jam puffs, 1 large cold plum-pudding (this must be good), a few baskets of fresh fruit, 3 dozen plain biscuits, a piece of cheese, 6 lbs. of butter (this, of course, includes the butter for tea), 4 quartern loaves of household bread, 3 dozen rolls, 6 loaves of tin bread (for tea), 2 plain plum cakes, 2 pound cakes, 2 sponge cakes, a tin of mixed biscuits, ½ lb. of tea. Coffee is not suitable for a picnic, being difficult to make.

Beverages.—3 dozen quart bottles of ale, packed in hampers; ginger-beer, soda-water, and lemonade, of each 2 dozen bottles; 6 bottles of sherry, 6 bottles of claret, champagne à discrétion, and any other light wine that may be preferred, and 2 bottles of brandy. Water can usually be obtained so it is useless to take it.

MRS BEETON *Beeton's Book of Household Management* 1861

Victorian Abundance

*Pheasant and a raised pie go to make up a substantial repast with a
Victorian flavour. Finish with a traditional summer pudding.*

Crumbed Pheasant Pieces

This is a classic hunt breakfast dish. If pheasant isn't
available, chicken, duck, turkey or guinea fowl will do.

Serves 6

1 pheasant	1 sprig of rosemary
250 ml (8 fl oz) dry white	1 sprig of oregano
wine	Salt and pepper
1 onion, finely chopped	3 tablespoons sunflower
1 teaspoon celery seed	oil
1 clove of garlic, crushed	A dash of Tabasco
and minced	2 eggs, beaten
2 cloves	75 g (3 oz) savoury
1 bay leaf	biscuit crumbs

Cut as much meat as possible off the bird, leaving bones
in where necessary. Cut or trim the pieces into finger-
sized portions.

In a large bowl, combine the wine, onion, celery seed,
garlic, cloves, bay leaf, rosemary, oregano, and salt and
pepper to taste. Submerge and toss the pheasant pieces.
Allow to marinate overnight.

Preheat the oven to 180°C/350°F/gas mark 4. Oil a baking
tray. Remove the pheasant pieces from the marinade,
drain them and pat them dry. Reserve about one-quarter
of the marinade and beat with the Tabasco and the eggs.
Spread the biscuit crumbs on a plate. Dip the pheasant
pieces in the egg and then in the crumbs, arrange them
on the baking tray and cover them with foil. Bake them
for 45 minutes, then uncover them and bake for a
further 10 minutes or so, till they are brown. Cool and
pack into a plastic box.

Raised Minced Pie

An adaptation of a Victorian recipe. Don't let the
quantities of meat quoted in the recipe limit your
imagination: increase the proportion of pork, if you like
– or replace the pork with beef, for a change.

Serves 6 to 8

For the pastry	For the filling
450 g (1 lb) plain flour	350 g(12 oz) minced pork
2 teaspoons salt	350 g(12 oz) minced
100 g (4 oz) lard	veal
275 ml (9 fl oz) boiling	350 g (12 oz) minced ham
water	¼ teaspoon crumbled
1 egg, beaten	dried sage
	Salt and pepper
	150 ml (¼ pint) stock

Make the pastry first. Sift the flour and salt into a bowl.
Put the lard and the boiling water in a saucepan and
heat gently to melt the lard. Pour the liquid into the
centre of the flour, beat with a wooden spoon till all the
ingredients are combined, then, using your hand and
the spoon, work the dough till it is firm, elastic and
satiny. Cover it with plastic film and leave it to rest in the
fridge for about 30 minutes.

Meanwhile, place all the meat in a large bowl, add the
sage, and salt and pepper to taste, and mix well.

Cut off about a quarter of the pastry and reserve it. Take
the rest and roll it out into a large circle. Now take a
large straight-sided jar (900 g/2 lb size). Turn the jar
upside down and press the pastry over it, working it up
the sides. Turn the jar back on its base, place it on a
baking sheet and gradually slide it out of the pastry.
Reshape the pastry case if necessary, then fill.

Wrap a doubled strip of greaseproof paper, about 5 cm (2 in) in depth, around the lower part of the pastry case; secure it with pins. The major part of the case should show above the paper.

Preheat the oven to 190°C/375°F/gas mark 5. Roll out the remaining pastry to a thickness of about 2 cm (¾ in), to make a lid for the pie. Brush the pastry lid with a little of the beaten egg, and press it on top of the pie, pinching the edges. Make a hole in the centre for steam to escape. Brush the top with egg and, if you like, decorate it with pastry cut-outs.

Bake the pie for 45 minutes, then reduce the heat to 150°C/300°F/gas mark 2 and bake for a further 45 minutes. About 20 minutes before the end of cooking remove the greaseproof paper strip and let the pie finish baking with the sides uncovered, so that they crisp. When the pie is golden take it from the oven and allow it to cool.

Meanwhile, bring the stock to the boil, then allow it to cool, but make sure it remains liquid. Pour the stock into the pie through the hole in the lid. Chill the pie to set the stock to a jelly.

Take the pie to the picnic wrapped in a clean tea towel.

Summer Pudding

Serves 6

1 loaf thick-sliced white bread
100 g (4 oz) redcurrants
50 g (2 oz) blackcurrants
350 g (12 oz) raspberries
175 g (6 oz) strawberries, halved
100 g (4 oz) brown sugar

Line a medium-sized baking dish or soufflé dish with as many bread slices as are needed. Put all the fresh berries in a large saucepan with the sugar and heat gently till they just begin to stew. Remove from the heat, spoon off some of the juices, and put the rest of the juices and all the fruit into the bread-lined dish. Cover with more bread slices, fitting closely together. Put a weight on the top, and leave in the fridge to chill overnight.

Take the pudding to the picnic in its dish, and also take a large plate and, in another container, the additional juices. Unmould the pudding on to the plate, and ladle the juices over. Serve with dollops of clotted cream.

A Barbecue

*The barbecue is a simple and satisfying
method of cooking outside – as Mark Twain's
Tom and Huck found.*

They came back to camp wonderfully refreshed, glad-hearted, and ravenous;
and they soon had the camp-fire blazing up again. Huck found a spring of
clear cold water close by, and the boys made cups of broad oak or hickory
leaves, and felt that water, sweetened with such a wild-wood charm as that,
would be a good enough substitute for coffee. While Joe was slicing bacon for
breakfast, Tom and Huck asked him to hold on a minute; they stepped to a
promising nook in the river bank and threw in their lines; almost immediately
they had reward. Joe had not had time to get impatient before they were back
again with some handsome bass, a couple of sun-perch, and a small catfish –
provision enough for quite a family. They fried the fish with the bacon and
were astonished; for no fish had ever seemed so delicious before. They did
not know that the quicker a freshwater fish is on the fire after he is caught the
better he is; and they reflected little upon what a sauce open-air sleeping,
open-air exercise, bathing, and a large ingredient of hunger make, too.

MARK TWAIN *The Adventures of Tom Sawyer* 1876

A Barbecue

*This barbecue offers a wealth of fresh-grilled, flavours, spicy and sweet.
The light cake, a combination of two golden summer fruits, provides the
perfect ending.*

Chillied Monkfish

Serves 6

*900 g (2 lb) monkfish,
 cleaned and trimmed
1 lemon, strained juice
60 ml (2 fl oz) sunflower
 oil
1 large onion, finely
 chopped
50 g (2 oz) fresh
 coriander, trimmed of
 stalks*

*8 cloves of garlic, chopped
1 tablespoon chopped
 fresh ginger
3 canned jalapeño
 chillies, drained and
 chopped
250 ml (8 fl oz) yogurt*

Cut the monkfish into 3.5 cm (1½ in) cubes. Put the
lemon juice, oil, onion, coriander, garlic, ginger and
chillies into the bowl of a blender or food processor,
and process to a purée.

Empty three-quarters of the purée into a large bowl and
add the monkfish. Toss the fish cubes to coat them
thoroughly. Cover and chill overnight.

Beat the remaining purée with the yogurt, and put in
another small bowl to chill overnight.

Before leaving for the picnic, take the monkfish from its
marinade and place the cubes on skewers, about 4
cubes to a skewer (use either small metal skewers or
wooden skewers which have first been soaked in water).
Transport the skewers to the picnic in a large plastic
box. Grill the fish over hot coals, about 5 minutes a side.
Serve with the yogurt-chilli dipping sauce.

Apple-Glazed Spare Ribs

Serves 6

2.25 kg (5 lb) spare ribs

For the marinade
*1 onion, thinly sliced
250 ml (8 fl oz) soy sauce
250 ml (8 fl oz) dry sherry
4 cloves of garlic, crushed
2 tablespoons grated
 horseradish
1 tablespoon Dijon
 mustard
1 tablespoon peeled and
 grated fresh ginger root
1 tablespoon grated
 lemon rind
1 tablespoon fresh lemon
 juice
A dash of Tabasco*

For the glaze
*6 tablespoons apple juice
6 tablespoons sugar
A dash of grated nutmeg
A dash of ground cloves
½ teaspoon cinnamon
1½ teaspoons cornflour*

Separate the spare ribs. Make the marinade. In a large
bowl, combine the onion, soy sauce, sherry, garlic,
horseradish, mustard, ginger root, lemon rind and juice
and Tabasco. Put all the spare ribs in the bowl and toss
to combine. Leave to marinate overnight, turning and
tossing occasionally.

To make the glaze, combine the apple juice and all the
other glaze ingredients in a small saucepan and bring to
the boil. Heat for about 5 minutes, till thickened. Pour
into a small container to carry to the picnic. Take a
basting brush as well.

Pack the spare ribs, drained of their marinade, in a large
plastic box. Grill them over hot coals for about 45
minutes, basting them occasionally with the glaze.

Charcoal-Roasted Vegetables

Serves 6

2 large aubergines,
    trimmed
Olive oil
4 medium onions
4 red or green sweet
    peppers

8 large tomatoes
Salt and pepper
Garlic butter
25 g (1 oz) Parmesan
    cheese, grated

Cut each aubergine lengthwise into 4 equal slices. Rub the cut sides with olive oil.

When the coals are covered in ash and are glowing, place a thin-meshed rack (such as the grill rack from your cooker) over the grill. Grease it with olive oil, and put the onions on it. Cook them for 15 minutes, turning them frequently, then add the aubergines and the whole peppers to the rack; 10 minutes later, add the tomatoes. Cook, turning fairly often, till the onions are tender when pierced with a knife, the aubergines are soft, the peppers are blistered all over, and the skins of the tomatoes have split. Remove the vegetables as they are done and keep them warm at the side of the barbecue.

Peel the onions and cut them in half. Slice the peppers. Arrange all the vegetables on a platter, and serve with seasoning, garlic butter, and Parmesan to sprinkle over.

Nectarine-Apricot Cake

Serves 6 to 8

2 eggs
125 ml (4 fl oz)
    sunflower oil
175 ml (6 fl oz)
    concentrated orange
    juice
3 nectarines, skinned and
    finely chopped
250 g (9 oz) plain flour
225 g (8 oz) brown sugar
1 teaspoon baking
    powder
½ teaspoon bicarbonate
    of soda

For the frosting
225 g (8 oz) cream cheese
100 g (4 oz) apricot jam
2 tablespoons icing sugar

Preheat the oven to 180°C/350°F/gas mark 4. Grease an 18 × 28 cm (7 × 11 in) cake tin. Using an electric mixer, beat together the eggs, oil and concentrated juice till the mixture is foamy. Stir in the chopped nectarines. In another bowl, mix together the dry ingredients. Slowly add to the egg mixture, stirring well.

Pour the cake batter into the prepared tin. Bake for about 45 minutes, or till the cake is golden and is pulling away from the sides of the tin. Let the cake cool in the tin.

To make the frosting, beat together all the frosting ingredients in a bowl. Spread over the top of the cooled cake with a palette knife. Transport the cake in its tin.

A Picnic for Two

Elliott Templeton insists that a picnic for lovers
must be nicely judged; his sister is less concerned.
For Laurence Whistler and his beloved wife,
the simplest of picnics sufficed.

'There are few things so pleasant as a picnic lunch eaten in perfect comfort,'
Elliott added sententiously. 'The old Duchesse d'Uzes used to tell me that the
most recalcitrant male becomes amenable to suggestion in these conditions.
What will you give them for luncheon?'

'Stuffed eggs and a chicken sandwich.'

'Nonsense. You can't have a picnic without *pâté de foie gras*. You must give
them curried shrimps to start with, breast of chicken in aspic with a heart-of-
lettuce salad for which I'll make the dressing myself, and after the *pâté* if you
like, as a concession to your American habits, an apple pie.'

'I shall give them stuffed eggs and a chicken sandwich, Elliott,' said Mrs
Bradley with decision.

'Well, mark my words, it'll be a failure and you'll only have yourself to
blame.'

W. SOMERSET MAUGHAM *The Razor's Edge* 1944

Then she would bring out a picnic lunch to me under the wall. Upright on her
haunches, eating a sandwich with both hands, back very straight, she looked
something like a red squirrel.

Through a sequence of bright days from April on into May, I wrote in the
slants of bluebells just above us . . . Here she would come with the lunch-
basket, sauntering in green skirt and sandals, lit or lost along the path through
patches of unpierced shade; in reverie, yet observant.

LAURENCE WHISTLER *The Initials in the Heart* 1964

A Picnic for Two

There is nothing more romantic than escaping to the countryside – just the two of you. The food should complement the mood: light but satisfying, with slightly unexpected overtones.

Green Eggs and Mozzarella Tomatoes

Serves 2

2 eggs, hard-boiled and shelled
25 g (1 oz) watercress, very finely chopped
2 teaspoons softened butter
3 heaped tablespoons ricotta cheese
Salt
Freshly ground black pepper

Cayenne pepper
2 beefsteak tomatoes
100 g (4 oz) mozzarella cheese, cut in small cubes
1 tablespoon chopped basil
2 tablespoons vinaigrette dressing (see page 25)

Cut the eggs in half lengthwise. Scoop out the yolks and press them through a sieve into a bowl. Stew the watercress gently in the butter, then scrape into the bowl with the yolks. Add the ricotta cheese. With a fork, mash the eggs, watercress and cheese together till the mixture is as smooth as possible. Season to taste with salt, black pepper and cayenne. Pile the mixture into the four egg whites, press decoratively with the fork and sprinkle with a little more cayenne. Cover and chill.

Cut the tops off the beefsteak tomatoes and, with a spoon, scoop out the insides. Turn the tomato shells upside down to drain, and put the flesh into a small sieve to drain. Then finely chop the flesh and mix with the cubed cheese in a small bowl; stir in the basil and the vinaigrette dressing. Cover and chill for a couple of hours. Then stuff the tomatoes with the cheese and tomato filling, drained of the vinaigrette marinade.

Pack the eggs and the tomatoes in a plastic box.

Salmon Terrine with Green Sauce

For the terrine
225 g (½ lb) salmon or salmon trout
100 g (4 oz) haddock
White pepper to taste
1 large egg
2 large egg whites
50 g (2 oz) butter, softened and cut into small pieces
300 ml (½ pint) double cream
550 g (1¼ lb) fillets of sole

For the sauce
1 bunch of watercress, finely chopped
4 spring onions, finely chopped
A small handful of fresh basil leaves, finely chopped
6 tablespoons mayonnaise
4 tablespoons double cream, whipped
Salt and pepper

To make this terrine, you really need a food processor – or diligent kitchen staff! Put the plastic bowl and metal blade of the food processor to chill in the fridge for about an hour. Meanwhile, pat dry the salmon and haddock and chop them roughly. Assemble the food processor and put in the chopped fish with pepper to taste. Run the machine for about half a minute, then while continuing to run it add the egg and egg whites through the feed tube. When they are blended in, add the butter. Mix till thoroughly combined. Add the cream little by little through the tube. The mixture should be airy.

Preheat the oven to 200°C/400°F/gas mark 6.

Cut the sole fillets into thin strips. Spread about a third of the fish mousse in a layer on the bottom of an ovenproof terrine. Lay half of the sole strips on it. Cover with another third of the mousse, top that with the remaining sole strips, and finish with the remaining mousse.

Cover the terrine with foil and place it in a larger pan; pour hot water into the larger pan till it comes half-way up the sides of the terrine. Bake for about 45 minutes, till the terrine is firm. Cool thoroughly before unmoulding.

While the terrine is baking, make the sauce. Place the watercress, the spring onions and the basil leaves in the food processor. Purée, then – with the machine running – add the mayonnaise. Turn the purée into another bowl and gently fold in the whipped cream. Season to taste.

Cut slices of terrine for two and place in a plastic container, saving the remainder to eat over the next few days as a happy reminder of your picnic. Take the sauce in a separate bottle.

Chicken Salad Mauritian with Lime Mayonnaise

Serves 2, generously

450 ml (¾ pint) chicken broth	*For the mayonnaise*
1 bay leaf	*1 large egg*
4 parsley sprigs, chopped	*5 teaspoons fresh lime juice*
Salt and pepper	*¼ teaspoon salt*
2 whole chicken breasts (about 675 g/1½ lb), each chopped in half	*2 teaspoons prepared mustard*
2 stalks celery, trimmed and chopped	*¼ teaspoon cayenne pepper*
1 can lychees, drained and halved	*250 ml (8 fl oz) sunflower oil*
50 g (2 oz) walnuts, chopped	
⅓ teaspoon grated fresh lime rind	
A small handful of parsley, trimmed of stalks and finely chopped	

Pour the broth into a saucepan, add the bay leaf and the chopped parsley, season with salt and pepper and bring to the boil. Lower the heat and add the chicken pieces to the broth. Cook at a bare simmer for about 8 minutes. Remove from the heat and let the chicken stand in the broth for a further 25 minutes. Remove the chicken, pat dry, and cut into small pieces. Place the pieces in a large bowl. Reserve the broth for another use.

Add the celery, lychees, walnuts, lime rind and parsley to the chicken in the bowl. Toss lightly.

Meanwhile, make the mayonnaise. Whisk the egg with the lime juice, salt and mustard and cayenne until they are all thoroughly combined. Whisking all the time, add the oil, first drop by drop, then in a thin stream. Whisk till all the oil is incorporated and the mayonnaise is emulsified.

Fold the mayonnaise gently into the salad. Transfer the salad to a large plastic bowl or box, cover, and chill until needed.

Coeurs à la Crème

Serves 2

150 ml (¼ pint) double cream, whipped	*1 egg white, stiffly beaten*
225 g (8 oz) cream cheese or curd cheese	*225 g (8 oz) fresh strawberries, hulled (use wild strawberries, if available)*
1 tablespoon caster sugar	

Line two small pierced heart-shaped moulds with muslin. Mix the cream with the cheese in a bowl, and stir in the sugar. Fold in the egg white gently. Press the mixture into the lined moulds, and leave to drain overnight.

Transport the little puddings to the picnic in their moulds and the strawberries in a separate container. To serve, turn out the two hearts on to small plates and surround them with the strawberries.

White Sangria

Serves 2

1 bottle Sancerre or Vouvray	*10 seedless white grapes*
2 tablespoons Cointreau or Grand Marnier	*2 orange slices, halved*
1 tablespoon sugar	*½ green apple, roughly chopped*
	5 strawberries, halved

Combine the wine, Cointreau and sugar in a jug and stir. Add the grapes, orange slices, apple and strawberries. Chill, covered, for at least 3 hours, stirring occasionally to combine flavours. Transport to the picnic in a wide-necked vacuum flask.

A Simple Picnic

An impromptu snack on the grass,
or cup of tea by the roadside,
are two of the most dependable
of life's simple pleasures.

Having climbed to a dry slope among the pepper-bushes, the party fell on the contents of the lunch-basket. . . .early rising and hard scrambling had whetted the appetites of the naturalists, and the nursery fare which Cicely spread before them seemed a sumptuous reward for their toil.

'I do like this kind of picnic much better than the ones where mother takes all the footmen, and the mayonnaise has to be scraped off things before I can eat them,' Cicely declared, lifting her foaming mouth from a beaker of milk.

EDITH WHARTON *The Fruit of the Tree* 1907

The evening was quite splendid, the sky yellow and pink, and the distant hills coming out soft and blue, both behind and in front of us. We changed horses at the *Spital,* and about two miles beyond it – at a place called *Loch-na-Braig* – we stopped, and while Grant ran back to get from a small house some hot water in the kettle, we three, with Brown's help, scrambled over a low stone wall by the roadside, and lit a fire and prepared our tea. The kettle soon returned, and the hot tea was very welcome and refreshing.

QUEEN VICTORIA *More Leaves from the Journal of a Life in the Highlands* 6.10.1866

A Simple Picnic

A simple picnic, to sustain walkers or riders: a soup which can be drunk hot or cold, savoury sandwiches with a touch of the unexpected – and a cake that is a legacy from the nineteenth-century sea captains who used to sail the whalers along the New England coast.

Carrot and Orange Soup

Serves 4 to 6

450 g (1 lb) carrots, finely chopped
1 medium onion, finely chopped
50 g (2 oz) butter
900 ml (1½ pints) chicken stock (or use thinned chicken consommé)
A bouquet garni
Salt and pepper
2 oranges, strained juice

Sweat the carrots and the onion in the butter for 10 minutes. Add the stock, bouquet garni and seasoning; cover and simmer for 40 minutes.

Liquidize the soup in batches. If it is to be served hot, return it to the saucepan. Stir in the orange juice and reheat the soup gently – do not allow it to boil. Decant into a warmed vacuum flask.

If the soup is to be served cold, pour it from the liquidizer into a jug, stir in the juice, allow it to cool thoroughly, then chill it in the fridge. Decant into a vacuum flask.

Olive Rye Bread Tuna Sandwiches

Makes 6 sandwiches

For the bread
15 g (½ oz) fresh yeast
125 ml (4 fl oz) lukewarm water
3 tablespoons molasses
1 teaspoon instant coffee
1 teaspoon salt
150 g (5 oz) rye flour
½ tablespoon yeast extract
175 g (6 oz) wholemeal flour
175 g (6 oz) plain white flour
½ tablespoon sunflower oil
50 g (2 oz) black olives, pitted and chopped
2 teaspoons cold water
1 egg white

For the filling
400–425 g (14–15 oz) tuna in oil, drained (2 cans)
3 stalks celery, finely chopped
2 large gherkins, finely chopped
1 egg, hard-boiled and finely chopped
20 green olives, pitted and finely chopped
150 ml (¼ pint) mayonnaise

Make the bread. In a large bowl, cream the yeast with a little of the warm water, then stir in the molasses and the rest of the warm water. Let this mixture stand for about 10 to 12 minutes, till it is foamy.

Stir in the instant coffee, the salt, the rye flour and the yeast extract. Add the wholemeal flour and half of the plain white flour and work to make a sticky dough.

Let the dough rest for 5 or 10 minutes. Then add the remaining flour little by little, working and kneading it into the dough. (Even when all the flour has been worked in the dough will be quite sticky.) Roll the dough in the sunflower oil, cover with a damp tea towel and leave to rise for about 3 hours, till it has doubled in bulk.

Sprinkle the chopped olives over the dough, and work and roll and knead till they are all incorporated. Shape the dough into an oblong loaf. Sprinkle a little flour on a baking tray. Roll the loaf in the flour, then set it on the tray. Leave it to rise till it has again doubled in bulk.

Preheat the oven to 200°C/400°F/gas mark 6. Beat together the egg white and the cold water and brush the loaf with it. Bake the loaf for about 30 minutes, till it is dark in colour and the bottom sounds hollow when it is tapped. Set it on a wire rack to cool thoroughly before you slice it for the sandwiches.

Meanwhile, make the tuna filling: mash the tuna in a bowl till it has the consistency of a paste. Mix in the chopped celery, gherkins, egg, and olives, then stir in the mayonnaise.

Slice the bread into 12 thin slices. Spread 6 of the slices with the tuna mixture, and cover with the remaining 6 slices. Cut into halves or quarters. Wrap in plastic film to transport.

Devilled Egg Sandwiches

Makes 4 sandwiches

*5 eggs, hard-boiled and
  shelled
5 slices streaky bacon,
  fried, rinds removed
60 ml (2 fl oz)
  mayonnaise
1 teaspoon Worcestershire
  sauce
2 teaspoons mild prepared
  mustard*

*2 drops Tabasco or red
  pepper sauce
A large pinch of curry
  powder
A pinch of cayenne pepper
8 slices of brown bread
Butter, softened
Mango chutney*

Chop the eggs and the bacon and place in a bowl. Spoon in the mayonnaise, Worcestershire sauce, mustard, Tabasco, curry powder and cayenne. Mix together thoroughly.

Butter the slices of bread, and on 4 of them spread mango chutney to taste. Top the chutney with the egg mixture, spreading it out evenly over the 4 slices. Top with the remaining bread, and cut into halves or quarters. Wrap in plastic film to transport.

Apple Sauce Cake

The original recipe specifies chicken fat, but ordinary vegetable oil will do.

Makes a 20 cm (8 in) cake

*3 cooking apples, peeled,
  cored and roughly
  chopped
½ tablespoon lemon juice
½ cup water
15 g (½ oz) butter
175 g (6 oz) raisins
50 g (2 oz) hazel nuts
1 small bottle maraschino
  cherries, thoroughly
  drained
1 teaspoon bicarbonate of
  soda*

*125 ml (4 fl oz) rendered
  chicken fat, or vegetable
  oil
225 g (8 oz) light brown
  sugar
200 g (7 oz) plain white
  flour
½ teaspoon salt
1 teaspoon cinnamon
½ teaspoon nutmeg
¼ teaspoon powdered
  cloves*

Make the apple sauce. Put the chopped apples in a saucepan with the lemon juice and water, bring to the boil, and simmer till the apples are soft – about 15 minutes. Beat well, to reduce the apples to a purée, then stir in the butter. You should have about 225 g (8 oz) of apple sauce. Reserve.

Mix the raisins, nuts and cherries and put them through a mincer, or, alternatively, chop them finely in a food processor. They should be in very tiny pieces, and well combined, but not an amorphous paste. Reserve.

Preheat the oven to 180°C/350°F/gas mark 4. Grease a 20 cm (8 in) square cake tin.

In a large bowl, stir the bicarbonate of soda and the apple sauce together, and then stir in the fat or oil and the sugar. Mix in the flour, salt and spices, and finally add the ground fruit and nut mixture. Combine thoroughly.

Pour the cake mixture into the tin and bake for 1 to 1¼ hours, till a fine skewer pushed into the middle comes out clean. Allow the cake to cool in the tin for 10 minutes before turning it out on a wire rack to complete cooling. Wrap in foil or plastic film to transport.

Three Meals in a Boat

George, in Three Men in a Boat,
*has firm views on what is suitable fare
for a boating picnic.*

For other breakfast things, George suggested eggs and bacon which were easy to cook, cold meat, tea, bread and butter, and jam. For lunch, he said, we could have biscuits, cold meat, bread and butter, and jam – but *no cheese*. Cheese, like oil, makes too much of itself. It wants the whole boat to itself. It goes through the hamper, and gives a cheesy flavour to everything else there. You can't tell whether you are eating apple pie, or German sausage, or strawberries and cream. It all seems cheese. There is too much odour about cheese. 'We shan't want any tea,' said George (Harris's face fell at this); 'but we'll have a good round, square, slap-up meal at seven – dinner, tea and supper combined.'

Harris grew more cheerful. George suggested meat and fruit pies, cold meat, tomatoes, fruit, and green stuff. For drink, we took some wonderful sticky concoction of Harris's, which you mixed with water and called lemonade, plenty of tea, and a bottle of whisky, in case, as George said, we got upset.

JEROME K. JEROME *Three Men in a Boat* 1889

Three Meals in a Boat

A jolly picnic for the young at heart. And just in case of upset, you are armed with an upside-down cake!

Baby Tomatoes with Two Stuffings

Enough for 6

20 cherry tomatoes	*175 g (6 oz) tuna*
3 stalks celery, finely chopped	*1½ tablespoons mayonnaise*
75 g (3 oz) cream cheese	*1½ tablespoons chopped parsley*
2 teaspoons lemon juice	
Salt and pepper	*Salt and pepper*

Wash and dry the tomatoes and remove the stalks. Cut a little slice off the bottom of each one so that they stand upright, then slice off the tops cleanly. Use a small coffee spoon to scrape out the seeds and the pulp. Place the tomato shells upside down on a draining board or a small mesh rack and allow them to drain for about an hour. Then store them upside down in the fridge till you are ready to stuff them.

Mix the chopped celery with the cream cheese and 1 teaspoon of the lemon juice. Season with salt and pepper to taste and use to fill half the tomatoes.

Mix the tuna with the mayonnaise, the parsley and the other teaspoon of lemon juice. Mash with a fork into a paste, and season with salt and pepper. Spoon the mixture into the remaining 10 tomatoes.

To transport, pack all the tomatoes tightly in a plastic box with a lid.

Partridge and Pigeon Pâté

This pâté may seem extravagant, but it makes a substantial main course for 8. It is worth making in this quantity even if there are only 3 or 4 men in your picnic boat, as any that is left over will keep for several days, and provide an impressive first course for another meal. Just pat down any ruffled edges, seal with melted butter, and store in the fridge.

Serves 8

4 partridges, plucked, cleaned and trussed	*150 ml (¼ pint) double cream*
2 pigeons, plucked, cleaned and trussed	*2 tablespoons dry sherry*
175 g (6 oz) bacon, chopped	*1 tablespoon Worcestershire sauce*
1 onion, chopped	*8 rashers of streaky bacon*
100 g (4 oz) butter	

Preheat the oven to 200°C/400°F/gas mark 6. Make sure that all stray feathers have been plucked from the birds; wash them and pat them dry. Melt the butter in a large roasting tin, and sauté the chopped bacon and onion over a gentle heat till the onion is just coloured. Quickly brown the pigeons, then remove them from the tin and brown the partridges in the same way. When the partridges have been browned, baste them and cover the tin. Put the tin in the oven and roast the partridges for 10 minutes. Then take the lid from the tin, add the pigeons, cover the tin again and continue to roast for a further 30 minutes. Take the birds from the oven and allow them to cool.

When they are cool enough to handle, remove the skins and discard them. Then carefully remove the meat from the bones. Reserve about 12 slices of partridge meat. Put the rest of the meat, together with the bacon and juices from the tin, into a blender or food processor, and blend till you have a fairly smooth mixture. Add the cream, sherry and Worcestershire sauce and continue to blend.

Preheat the oven to 190°C/375°F/gas mark 5. Grease the sides of a deep terrine or baking dish. Take a third of the pâté, spread it over the bottom of the dish and place half the reserved partridge slices on top. Cover with another third of the pâté, put the rest of the partridge slices on top, then cover with the remainder of the pâté. Lay the streaky bacon slices over the top. Bake the pâté for 25 minutes, allow it to cool thoroughly, then chill.

Transport the pâté to the picnic in its dish. Serve with generous slices of French bread.

Lettuce and New Pea Salad

This classic combination provides a clean-tasting foil for the pâté. The baby peas are lightly pickled in their vinaigrette seasoning.

Serves 6

6 hearts of lettuce, washed
   and trimmed
900 g (2 lb) new peas,
   shelled, cooked, drained
   and cooled
A large handful of fresh
   mint, finely chopped
Salt and pepper

For the dressing
1 teaspoon Dijon mustard
1 tablespoon white wine
   vinegar
1 teaspoon honey
3 tablespoons sunflower
   oil

Tear the lettuce hearts into small pieces and place in the container to go to the picnic. Toss with the cooled baby peas and the fresh mint. Season to taste.

In a bottle, combine the mustard, vinegar, honey and sunflower oil. Cover and shake until thoroughly combined. Bring the bottle with the dressing to the picnic and toss the salad just before serving.

Pineapple Upside-Down Cake

Makes a 23 cm (9 in) cake

225 g (8 oz) butter
225 g (8 oz) dark brown
   sugar
60 ml (2 fl oz) pineapple
   juice
5 pineapple rings
5 glacé cherries
1 egg

125 ml (4 fl oz) milk
200 g (7 oz) plain white
   flour
2 teaspoons baking
   powder
½ teaspoon salt
100 g (4 oz) caster sugar

Preheat the oven to 200°C/400°F/gas mark 6. Melt one-third of the butter in a 23 cm (9 in) round cake tin, set over a low heat. Make sure the butter is evenly distributed. Still over the heat, stir in the brown sugar, and continue to stir until it dissolves. Take off the heat and pour in the pineapple juice, turning the tin around to coat it evenly. Place the pineapple rings in one layer in the bottom of the pan, and pop a glacé cherry into the centre of each ring. Set aside.

In a small saucepan, melt the remaining butter. Remove from the heat and beat in the egg and the milk. In a bowl, stir together the flour, baking powder, salt and sugar. Beat in the liquid mixture, to make a smooth batter. Pour over the pineapple slices in the cake tin and bake for about 35 to 40 minutes, until a fine skewer pushed into the centre comes out clean. Remove the cake from the oven and leave it to cool in the tin for some time before turning it out on to a plate, fruit-side up. Allow to cool completely before wrapping it in plastic film to take it on the picnic.

A Pickwickian Picnic

The members of the Pickwick Club, as you would expect,
really know how to enjoy a picnic.
Sam Weller unpacks the basket.

'Weal pie,' said Mr Weller, soliloquising, as he arranged the eatables on the grass. 'Wery good thing is weal pie, when you know the lady as made it, and is quite sure it an't kittens . . . Tongue; well, that's a wery good thing when it an't a woman's. Bread – knuckle o'ham, reg'lar picter – cold beef in slices, wery good. What's in them stone jars, young touch-and-go?'

'Beer in this one,' replied the boy, taking from his shoulder a couple of large stone bottles, fastened together by a leathern strap – 'cold punch in t'other.'

'And a wery good notion of a lunch it is, take it altogether,' said Mr Weller, surveying his arrangement of the repast with great satisfaction. 'Now gen'l'm'n, "fall on," as the English said to the French when they fixed bagginets.'

It needed no second invitation to induce the party to do full justice to the meal. . .

'This is delightful – thoroughly delightful!' said Mr Pickwick, the skin of whose expressive countenance was rapidly peeling off, with exposure to the sun.

'So it is: so it is, old fellow,' replied Wardle. 'Come; a glass of punch!'

'With great pleasure,' said Mr Pickwick; the satisfaction of whose countenance, after drinking it, bore testimony to the sincerity of the reply.

'Good,' said Mr Pickwick, smacking his lips. 'Very good. I'll take another. Cool; very cool. Come, gentlemen,' continued Mr Pickwick, still retaining his hold upon the jar, 'a toast. Our friends at Dingley Dell.'

The toast was drunk with loud acclamations.

CHARLES DICKENS *The Posthumous Papers of the Pickwick Club* 1837

A Pickwickian Picnic

This is the picnic to take to the races, or a point-to-point. In Victorian fashion, it is heavy with meat and fish: add plenty of fresh and crunchy vegetables, and lettuce to clear the palate. The Victorians loved the juxtaposition of sweet and sour, strong with mild. Some of these complementary opposites are re-created here.

Vinegared Salmon

Serves 6

6 salmon cutlets	10 peppercorns
150 ml (¼ pint) white wine	2 bay leaves
600 ml (1 pint) sherry vinegar	16 cardamom seeds
1 teaspoon salt	1 lemon, strained juice and grated rind

Preheat the oven to 190°C/375°F/gas mark 5. Place a large piece of foil on a baking tray and turn up its edges. Put the cutlets on the foil, brush them with oil and pour over the wine. Pull the foil over the fish and seal the edges so that the cutlets are completely enclosed. Bake for 25 minutes. Remove the parcel from the oven, open the foil and let the fish cool.

In a saucepan, combine the vinegar, salt, peppercorns, bay leaves, cardamom seeds and lemon juice and rind. Strain off the cooking juices of the fish and add to the vinegar. Bring to the boil, then reduce the heat and simmer for 10 minutes. Allow the liquid to cool.

Arrange the cutlets in a single layer in a rimmed dish. Pour the marinade over them and cover the dish. Leave the cutlets to marinate for at least 12 hours, turning them in the marinade from time to time.

To transport the fish to the picnic, transfer it, together with its marinade, to a large plastic box. Serve with slices of black bread.

Veal and Ham Pie

Serves 6 to 8

900 g (2 lb) pie veal	1 teaspoon chopped fresh thyme
225 g (8 oz) ham	1 teaspoon chopped fresh parsley
Hot-water pastry made with 450g (1 lb) flour (see page 44)	A pinch of allspice
1 medium onion, finely chopped	Salt and pepper
1 teaspoon anchovy paste	1 egg, beaten
	300 ml (½ pint) stock

Preheat the oven to 200°C/400°F/gas mark 6. Grease a 15 cm (6 in) round tin with a removable base. Chop the veal and the ham into small cubes. Reserve. Set aside a quarter of the pastry and roll out the remainder into a circle large enough to line the tin. In a large bowl mix the cubed veal and ham, the onion, the anchovy paste and the herbs, spices and seasonings. Pile the filling into the centre of the pastry-lined tin and press into the sides, so that it is evenly distributed. Roll out the rest of the pastry to make a lid, lay it on top of the pie, and cut a hole in the centre. Brush with the beaten egg.

Bake the pie in the hot oven for 30 minutes, then reduce the heat to 160°C/325°F/gas mark 3, and bake for a further 1½ hours.

Remove the pie from the oven and let it cool in the tin for 1 hour. Then remove it from the tin. Melt the stock, allow it to cool a little, and, using a funnel, pour it through the central hole of the pie. Chill to set the stock. Take the pie to the picnic wrapped in a clean tea towel.

Auntie Doris's Brisket of Beef with Anchovy Cream

Serves 8 to 10

1.75 to 2.25 kg (4 to 5 lb)
  brisket of beef
Salt and pepper
1.4 litres (2½ pints) beef
  dripping
2 bay leaves, crumbled

For the sauce
1 large clove of garlic
1 large egg
2 tablespoons lemon juice
2 teaspoons anchovy paste
60 ml (2 fl oz) beef stock
1 teaspoon prepared
  mustard
200 ml (7 fl oz) sunflower
  oil
90 ml (3 fl oz) soured
  cream

Preheat the oven to 150°C/300°F/gas mark 2. Season the joint with salt and pepper — being rather liberal with the latter. In a large casserole, melt down the beef dripping. Add the crumbled bay leaves. Place the beef joint in the liquid dripping: there should be enough to cover the meat. Cover the casserole tightly, put it in the oven and cook for about 45 minutes per 450 g (1 lb) of meat, with an extra 10 minutes at the end.

Carefully lift the meat from the fat with a carving fork. Hold it over the sink and pour a kettle of boiling water over it, turning the joint so that all excess fat is rinsed off. (An assistant is useful during this operation!) Transfer the meat to a large platter with a rim. Put a large board or plate on top of the meat and top with weights (a collection of tins and bags of sugar will do nicely). Leave overnight in a cool place. Remove the board and weights and transfer to a portable container. Slice the meat at the picnic – it will be meltingly tender.

The old-fashioned method of making the sauce entails a lot of pounding and beating. With modern equipment it is much easier. Boil the unpeeled garlic clove for about 10 minutes in a small saucepan. Peel it and chop it finely. Put the garlic, egg, lemon juice, anchovy paste, beef stock and mustard in the bowl of a blender or food processor and process until they are thoroughly combined. Add the oil in a thin stream, processing till the sauce is emulsified. Spoon in the soured cream and process till that too is all incorporated.

Transport the sauce in a separate container and serve as an accompaniment to the slices of cold brisket.

Old-Fashioned Trifle

Serves 6 to 8

8 sponge fingers
Strawberry jam
12 amaretti biscuits
8 coconut macaroons
8 or 9 tablespoons sherry
50 g (2 oz) blanched
  slivered almonds
1 lemon, grated rind

300 ml (½ pint) egg
  custard
2 egg whites
1½ tablespoons caster
  sugar
300 ml (½ pint) double
  cream, whipped
Glacé cherries and other
  candied fruits

If you can, use a light but pretty glass bowl, to show off the layers of the trifle. Split the sponge fingers in half lengthwise and spread them with jam; sandwich together again. Place 4 fingers in the bottom of the bowl, cover with half of the amaretti biscuits, then half of the macaroons, and then repeat the layers. It doesn't matter if, because of the shape of the bowl, the biscuits overlap. Pour over the sherry, trying to reach all the cake and biscuits. Sprinkle with the slivered almonds and the lemon rind, then pour over the cold custard. Whip the egg whites with the sugar till they hold stiff peaks. Gently fold them into the whipped cream, and pile the mixture on to the custard. Decorate with the glacé cherries and other candied fruits. Chill till you take to the picnic.

Classic Fare

*It is during a picnic on the river,
that Harriet Vane recognizes that she is
in love with Lord Peter Wimsey.*

'You will find the tea-basket,' said Wimsey, 'behind you in the bows.'

They had put in under the dappled shade of an overhanging willow a little down the left bank of the Isis.

. . . he lapsed into silence, while she studied his half-averted face. Considered generally, as a façade, it was by this time tolerably familiar to her, but now she saw details, magnified as it were by some glass in her own mind. . . .

He looked up; and she was instantly scarlet, as though she had been dipped in boiling water. Through the confusion of her darkened eyes and drumming ears some enormous bulk seemed to stoop over her. Then the mist cleared. His eyes were riveted upon the manuscript again, but he breathed as though he had been running.

So, thought Harriet, it has happened. But it happened long ago. The only new thing that has happened is that now I have got to admit it to myself . . .

'Oh, my lost youth. Here are the ducks coming up for the remains of our sandwiches. Twenty-three years ago I fed these identical ducks with these identical sandwiches.'

'Ten years ago, I too fed them to bursting point.'

'And ten and twenty years hence the same ducks and the same undergraduates will share the same ritual feast . . . How fleeting are all human passions compared with the massive continuity of ducks.'

DOROTHY SAYERS *Gaudy Night* 1935

Classic Fare

These recipes have a timeless quality which will sustain you through an emotional crisis in a punt or a day on the moors.

Hunter's Broth

Serves 4 to 6

3 tablespoons unsalted butter
2 large Spanish onions, chopped
2 carrots, peeled and chopped
2 small turnips, peeled and chopped

8 cloves of garlic, peeled and chopped
1 litre (1¾ pints) beef stock (or 1½ cans beef consommé, thinned)
300 ml (½ pint) red wine
1 cup cooked rice
Salt and pepper

Melt the butter in a large saucepan set over a medium heat. Add the onions, carrots, turnips, and garlic and sauté over low heat for about 30 minutes, till they are tender and coloured. Pour in the beef stock and the wine, bring to the boil, then reduce the heat, cover the pan and simmer for about 30 minutes.

Strain the stock and return the broth to the saucepan. Add the cooked rice and simmer for another 10 to 15 minutes. Season to taste. Pour into a warmed vacuum flask to take to the picnic.

Cucumber and Tarragon Cheese Sandwiches

Makes 8 tiny sandwiches

1 tablespoon unsalted butter, softened
1 tablespoon cream cheese
1 teaspoon chopped fresh tarragon

4 thin slices of white bread, crusts removed
1 small cucumber, halved lengthwise, seeded and sliced paper-thin

Cream together the softened butter, the cream cheese and the chopped tarragon. Spread the mixture on the bread slices. Place the cucumber slices in an overlapping pattern on 2 of the slices, and place the other 2 slices on top. Cover and chill for 1 to 2 hours. Cut each sandwich into four triangles before packing for the picnic.

Venison Meatloaf Sandwiches

Makes 6 to 8 sandwiches

450 g (1 lb) lean venison,
  minced
450 g (1 lb) lean veal,
  minced
225 g (8 oz) salt pork,
  finely chopped
2 tablespoons finely
  chopped onion
1 small carrot, finely
  chopped
1 small turnip, finely
  chopped
1 clove of garlic, finely
  chopped

50 g (2 oz) button
  mushrooms, chopped
50 g (2 oz) fresh
  breadcrumbs
Pepper
1 egg, lightly beaten
4 rashers of streaky bacon
1 loaf of soft brown
  granary bread
Mayonnaise
Tomato ketchup

Preheat the oven to 180°C/350°F/gas mark 5. In a large bowl, mix the venison, veal and salt pork together. With your hands, work the onion, carrot, turnip, garlic, mushrooms and breadcrumbs into the meat. Test for flavour, then add pepper to taste, and the egg, and continue to work till thoroughly combined. Shape into a loaf and place it in a shallow roasting tin. Fit the bacon rashers snugly around the loaf. Bake for 1 hour. Remove from the oven and allow to cool to room temperature.

Slice the granary bread – not too thinly – and spread half of the slices liberally with mayonnaise and the rest with tomato ketchup. Slice the meatloaf into thick pieces and sandwich each piece between a slice of bread spread with mayonnaise and one spread with ketchup. Wrap the sandwiches in plastic film to take to the picnic.

Real Scottish Shortbread

Makes 18 biscuits

225 g (8 oz) unsalted
  butter
100 g (4 oz) caster sugar
A pinch of salt

225 g (8 oz) plain white
  flour
A little extra caster sugar

Preheat the oven to 230°C/450°F/gas mark 8. Cream the butter and sugar together and add salt to taste. When the mixture is fluffy, mix in the flour, first using a fork, then the hands.

Press the shortbread dough into a 20 × 20 cm (8 × 8 in) ungreased cake tin. The dough should not be much thicker than ¼ to ⅓ in (5 to 8 mm). Prick all over with a fork. Bake in the hot oven for 10 minutes, then lower the heat to 180°C/350°F/gas mark 4 and bake for another 20 to 30 minutes, or till the shortbread is golden brown. Sprinkle the additional caster sugar all over the top, and cut through the pastry to make shortbread fingers. Allow to cool in the tin. The shortbread will keep for several weeks in an airtight tin, but is extra delicious when fresh.

Real Lemon Barley Water

Makes 3.5 litres (6 pints)

6 round, plump lemons
100 g (4 oz) pearl barley,
  washed and drained

100 g (4 oz) granulated
  sugar

Using a potato peeler, pare the rind very thinly off the fruit, making sure that there is no pith attached. Place the rind in a small saucepan with a thick base, and pour over just enough water to cover it. Bring to the boil, then turn down the heat and simmer for 5 or 6 minutes. Take off the heat and allow to cool slightly, then pour into a 4 litre (7 pint) jug or basin, or divide between two 2 litre (3½ pint) containers.

Place the barley in a large pot and cover well with water. Bring to the boil and boil for a few minutes, then drain the barley thoroughly and discard the water. Return the barley to the pot, cover with water again, rinse it well, and strain again, discarding the water. Put the barley in the container with the lemon rind, or if you are using two containers divide it equally between them.

Peel off and discard all the remaining pith on the 6 lemons. Cut the flesh into slices and place them in the container, or containers, with the barley and the rind. Pour the sugar into the small saucepan and cover it with water. Bring to the boil and cook until syrupy. Pour the syrup over the lemon-barley mixture. Bring another 3.5 litres (6 pints) of water to the boil, and pour over the lemon-barley mixture. Leave in a cold place, covered, overnight. Strain and bottle. This lemon barley water will keep for a week or two in the fridge or a cold place.

A Picnic Adventure

Eating outdoors is often an adventure in itself.
And if you can cook outdoors as well. . . .
In Swallows and Amazons, *the children have made a camp.*

In the open space under the trees the fire was burning merrily. The kettle had boiled, and was standing steaming on the ground. Susan was melting a big pat of butter in the frying pan. In a pudding-basin beside her she had six raw eggs. She had cracked the eggs on the edge of a mug and broken them into the basin. Their empty shells were crackling in the fire.

'No plates today,' said Mate Susan. 'We all eat out of the common dish.'

'But it isn't a common dish,' said Roger. 'It's a frying-pan.'

'Well, we eat out of it anyway.'

She had now emptied the raw eggs into the sizzling butter, and was stirring the eggs and the butter together after shaking the pepper pot over them, and putting in a lot of salt.

'They're beginning to curdle,' said Titty, who was watching carefully. 'When they begin to flake, you have to keep scraping them off the bottom of the pan. I saw Mrs Jackson do it.'

'They're flaking now,' said Susan. 'Come on and scrape away.'

She put the frying-pan on the ground, and gave everyone a spoon. The captain, mate and crew of the *Swallow* squatted round the frying-pan, and began eating as soon as the scrambled eggs, which were very hot, would let them. Mate Susan had already cut four huge slices of brown bread and butter to eat with the eggs. Then she poured out four mugs of tea. Then there were four big slabs of seed cake. Then there were apples all round.

ARTHUR RANSOME *Swallows and Amazons* 1930

70

A Picnic Adventure

This picaresque meal for young wanderers is lightweight, easy to carry and to digest.

Brilliant Bean Medley

Serves 6

For the salad
400 to 425 g (14 to 15 oz) can cooked chickpeas
400 to 425 g (14 to 15 oz) can cooked kidney beans
400 to 425 g (14 to 15 oz) can cooked white haricot beans
400 to 425 g (14 to 15 oz) can cooked black- eyed beans
25 g (8 oz) French beans, cooked and cut into thirds
3 stalks celery, cut into 2.5 cm (1 in) pieces
3 pimentoes, drained and cut into strips
1 onion, thinly sliced

For the dressing
1 egg yolk
1 tablespoon sugar
4 tablespoons red wine vinegar
1 clove of garlic, crushed
250 ml (8 fl oz) olive oil
Salt
Black pepper
Cayenne pepper

Thoroughly drain the canned chickpeas and all the canned beans. Rinse them in cold water and drain again. Mix together in a large bowl. Bring water to the boil in a saucepan, add the French beans, and cook for about 4 minutes. Drain and refresh under cold water; drain again. Add to the other beans. Stir in the celery, pimento strips and onion.

Make the dressing. Combine the egg yolk, sugar, wine vinegar and garlic in a blender or food processor. Process until mixed, then pour in the oil in a thin stream and process until emulsified. Add the salt, black pepper and cayenne to taste.

Toss the beans with the dressing and pack in a plastic box. If you have time, chill the dressed salad overnight – it will taste even better.

Scrambled Egg Salad

A creamy, delicious variation on the more usual hard-boiled egg salad.

Serves 6

10 large eggs
2 tablespoons butter
1 purple onion, finely chopped
5 sprigs fresh dill, trimmed, stalks removed
60 ml (2 fl oz) mayonnaise
30 ml (1 fl oz) soured cream

2 tablespoons Dijon mustard
Salt
Black pepper
Cayenne pepper
Rye bread toasts, cut into fingers

Beat the eggs with a fork. Melt the butter in a saucepan, over a low heat, and stir in the beaten eggs. Gently scramble the eggs, adjusting the temperature as necessary, till you have creamy curds, just set. Take the scrambled eggs off the heat, allow to cool slightly, and spoon them into a large bowl.

When the eggs have cooled to room temperature, add the onion and dill. In a small bowl, beat together the mayonnaise, soured cream and mustard, until thoroughly combined. Pour this sauce over the eggs, and gently fold it into them. Season with the salt, black pepper and cayenne. Transfer the egg salad to a plastic bowl or box. Pack the rye toasts in a separate box and serve them with the salad.

Seed Cake

Makes a 15 cm (6 in) square cake

100 to 150 g (4 to 5 oz)
    soft margarine
100 to 150 g (4 to 5 oz)
    caster sugar
2 eggs

225 g (8 oz) self-raising
    flour
2 teaspoons caraway
    seeds
2 to 3 tablespoons milk

Preheat the oven to 190°C/375°F/gas mark 5. Grease and flour a deep 15 × 15 cm (6 × 6 in) cake tin and line the bottom of the tin with greaseproof paper. Cream together the margarine and the sugar and beat in the eggs one at a time. Add a little of the measured flour if the mixture begins to curdle. Using a metal spoon, gently but thoroughly fold in the remaining flour. Finally stir in the caraway seeds and the milk.

Turn the mixture into the prepared tin, levelling the top. Bake for 90 minutes. If the cake seems to be cooking too quickly, lower the temperature to 180°C/350°F/gas mark 4. Turn out and cool on a wire rack. Take to the picnic in a plastic box.

Ruby Nectar

This is a version of a non-alcoholic cordial which has variations the world over. The Russians omit the ice and thicken the syrup with yogurt, while grown-up picnickers may prefer to add soda water – or even champagne.

225 g (8 oz) redcurrants,
washed and stripped
450 g (1 lb) raspberries,
washed

About 4 tablespoons sugar
1 lemon
Crushed ice

Place the redcurrants and raspberries in a saucepan (not aluminium), with a little water. Bring slowly to the boil, gently crushing and stirring the currants and berries, then add sugar to taste. Simmer for 5 to 10 minutes, till the fruits have given up their juices. Allow to cool.

Drain the syrupy juice through a fine nylon sieve into a jug. Squeeze in the juice of the lemon, then cover and chill till you are ready to go.

Just before leaving, pack 1 or 2 vacuum flasks with crushed ice, pour in the chilled syrup, and transport to the picnic.

Chocolate-Toffee Bars

Makes about 50 bars

225 g (8 oz) butter,
    softened
225 g (8 oz) sugar
1 egg yolk
200 g (7 oz) plain flour

450 g (1 lb) milk
    chocolate, broken into
    small pieces
50 g (2 oz) blanched
    slivered almonds

Preheat the oven to 150°C/300°F/gas mark 2. Grease a 25 × 38 cm (10 × 15 in) baking sheet. Combine the butter, sugar and egg yolk in a bowl, and beat until creamy. Add the flour and beat until the dough holds together.

With your hands, push and pat out the dough on the prepared baking sheet. Bake for between 50 minutes and an hour, until lightly golden.

Remove the pan from the oven, and scatter the chocolate pieces all over the pastry. When the chocolate begins to melt use a palette knife to spread it evenly over the pastry. Scatter the slivered almonds over. Let the chocolate-covered pastry cool until it is firm, then cut it into 4 × 7.5 cm (1½ × 3in) bars. Store in an airtight container. Pack in a plastic box to transport.

An Edwardian Idyll

'The past is a foreign country: they do things differently there.'
L.P. Hartley's memorable opening sentence casts a spell over
a story which has the enchanted clarity of a dream.

One remembers things at different levels. I still have an impression, distinct but hard to analyse, of the change that came over the household with Lord Trimingham's arrival. Before, it had had an air of self-sufficiency, and, in spite of Mrs Maudsley's hand on the reins, a go-as-you-please gait: now everyone seemed to be strung up, on tip-toe to face some test, as we were in the last weeks at school, with the examinations coming on. What one said and did seemed to matter more, as if something hung on it, as if it was contributing to a coming event.

That this had nothing to do with me I realized: the quickly summoned smiles, the suppressed anxiety, were not for me; in the conversation, which was never allowed to die away, I took little part. Picnics or expeditions or visits were planned for almost every day: Mrs Maudsley would announce them after breakfast; to the rest of us it sounded like a command, yet her eye would flash an interrogation at Lord Trimingham as if he were a signal that must be consulted before the train went on.

'Suits me down to the ground,' he would say, or, 'Just what I was hoping we should do.'

I can remember sitting by some stream and watching the hampers being unpacked, the rugs spread out, and the footman bending down to change our plates. The grown-ups drank amber wine out of tall tapering bottles; I was given fizzy lemonade from a bottle with a glass marble for a stopper. I enjoyed the meal; it was the conversation afterwards, while the things were being packed away, that was the strain. I got as near to Marian as I dared, but she did not look at me; she seemed to have eyes only for Lord Trimingham who sat beside her. I could not hear what they were saying to each other, and I knew I shouldn't have understood it if I had. I should have understood the words, of course, but not what made them say them.

L.P. Hartley *The Go-Between* 1953

An Edwardian Idyll

The Edwardians refined the art of the picnic, turning from the heavy pies and potted meats of the Victorians to more subtle fare.

Asparagus with Shallot Vinaigrette

Serves 6 to 7

40 to 45 spears of
    asparagus, trimmed

For the dressing
2 tablespoons tarragon
    vinegar
1 teaspoon sugar
200 ml (7 fl oz) olive oil
3 shallots, very finely
    chopped
Salt and pepper

First make the dressing. In a small bowl, beat together the vinegar and the sugar. Add the oil slowly, beating all the time, until the dressing is emulsified. Stir in the finely chopped shallots and salt and pepper to taste. Cover and leave for several hours, for the flavours to amalgamate.

Place the asparagus spears in a large saucepan, tips sticking out of the pan. If they look in danger of falling, tie them into bundles. Pour about 5 cm (2 in) of water into the pan. Cover the top of the pan and the tips of the asparagus with a domed piece of foil, secured to the top of the pan. Bring to the boil, then lower the heat and simmer for about 15 to 20 minutes, till the stalks are tender when pierced with a knife. Drain and allow to cool slightly. If the bottoms of the stems are still woody, trim them off.

Pack the asparagus spears into plastic boxes. Beat the dressing again briefly, and pour it over them. Cover and chill until it is time to go.

Glazed Ham Loaf

Serves 6 to 8

900 g (2 lb) gammon
    ham, minced
675 g (1½ lb) lean pork,
    minced
Salt and pepper
2 eggs, beaten
150 ml (¼ pint) milk
150 ml (¼ pint) single
    cream
50 g (2 oz) fresh brown
    breadcrumbs
1 tablespoon finely
    chopped parsley

For the glaze
350 g (12 oz) Demerara
    sugar
1 tablespoon Dijon
    mustard
150 ml (¼ pint) cider
    vinegar
6 tablespoons hot water

Preheat the oven to 180°C/350°F/gas mark 4. In a large bowl, combine the minced gammon and pork, and season carefully to taste – remember, the ham is salty already. With your hands, work in the eggs, milk, cream, breadcrumbs and parsley. Shape the mixture into a loaf, place on a shallow tray or baking tin, and roast in the oven for about 1½ hours.

To make the glaze, mix together the sugar, mustard, vinegar and water. When the loaf has started to brown, after about half an hour in the oven, baste with the sauce, and continue to baste at frequent intervals. When a fine skewer pushed into the loaf comes out clean, remove the loaf from the oven and allow it to cool. Pack it into a light, easily carried container to take it to the picnic. Serve with plenty of mustard.

Caramel and Ginger Cream

Serves 6

For the custard
4 eggs
2 egg yolks
50 g (2 oz) caster sugar
2 teaspoons ground
  ginger
300 ml (½ pint) milk
300 ml (½ pint) single
  cream

For the caramel
150 g (5 oz) Demerara
  sugar
2½ tablespoons water

Make the caramel first. Wipe the insides of six ramekins with a wet cloth. Set aside. Put the sugar, with the water, in a heavy-bottomed saucepan. Cook over a low heat, stirring frequently, until the sugar has dissolved, then stop stirring, increase the heat, and boil the syrup until it begins to turn a deep brown. Remove from the heat and pour some of the caramel into the bottom of each of the six ramekins, tilting them to distribute it evenly. Reserve.

Preheat the oven to 180°C/350°F/gas mark 4. Whisk the eggs and the extra yolks together, add the sugar and the ground ginger, and continue whisking until the mixture is smooth and pale. In a saucepan, heat the milk and cream until very hot but not quite boiling. Pour the hot mixture into the eggs in a thin stream, whisking continuously, until you have a smooth custard. Pour the custard into the six ramekins and cover them with foil. Place the ramekins in a large roasting pan and fill the pan with hot water to half-way up their sides. Bake for 40 to 45 minutes. Cool, then chill.

Transport the little custards to the picnic in the ramekins. To turn them out, run a knife carefully around the sides of each one, top with a plate, and turn over.

Brandied Peaches

About 5 peaches per jar
600 ml (1 pint) brandy
  per jar
Granulated sugar

This is very much an approximate recipe. Peel and stone the peaches and cut them in half. Pack the fruit into large jars, covering each layer with a thick topping of sugar. When each jar is full, pour over the brandy. If you can afford it, it is worth doing 3 or 4 jars at a time; they disappear as if by magic! Keep for several weeks before using.

Tea on the Lawn

Tea outdoors is one of the delights of summer.
Henry James writes of the charms of tea on an English lawn.
S.T. Aksakov describes a Russian picnic tea.

Under certain circumstances there are few hours in life more agreeable than the hour dedicated to the ceremony known as afternoon tea. There are circumstances in which, whether you partake of the tea or not – some people of course never do, – the situation is in itself delightful. Those that I have in mind . . . offered an admirable setting to an innocent pastime. The implements of the little feast had been disposed upon the lawn of an old English country house, in what I should call the perfect middle of a splendid summer afternoon. Part of the afternoon had waned, but much of it was left, and what was left was of the finest and rarest quality. Real dusk would not arrive for many hours; but the flood of summer light had begun to ebb, the air had grown mellow, the shadows were long upon the smooth, dense turf. They lengthened slowly, however, and the scene expressed that sense of leisure still to come which is perhaps the chief source of one's enjoyment of such a scene at such an hour. From five o'clock to eight is on certain occasions a little eternity; but on such an occasion as this the interval could be only an eternity of pleasure.

HENRY JAMES *The Portrait of a Lady* 1881

The horses were taken out and hobbled and allowed to crop the juicy young grass; a bright fire was lit, and the travelling samovar – really a large teapot with a funnel – was placed on it; a leather rug was spread out beside the carriage, the canteen was brought out, and tea served; how good it was in the fresh evening air!

S.T. AKSAKOV *A Russian Schoolboy* 1917

Tea on the Lawn

A traditional tea – with some differences, to awaken jaded palates. Whether you adopt Iced Rosehip and Redcurrant, or settle for a more familiar brew, all tea deserves to be made with care and drunk with relish.

Date Bread Sandwiches with Bacon and Cream Cheese

Makes 12 triangles

For the bread
175 g (6 oz) pitted and chopped dates
4 tablespoons unsalted butter, cut into small pieces
50 g (2 oz) soft brown sugar
50 g (2 oz) caster sugar
175 ml (6 fl oz) boiling water
1 egg, beaten
200 g (7 oz) plain white flour
2 teaspoons baking powder
½ teaspoon salt
½ teaspoon vanilla essence
1 tablespoon orange juice

For the filling
150 g (5 oz) cream cheese, softened
6 rashers of bacon, cooked until crispish, then finely chopped

Put the dates, the butter and the two types of sugar into a large bowl, and pour the boiling water over. Let stand for 8 minutes. Stir well to combine, then allow to cool to lukewarm.

Preheat the oven to 180°C/350°F/gas mark 4. Grease a 675 g (1½ lb) loaf tin. Stir the egg into the cooled date mixture, and then beat in the flour, baking powder and salt. Combine thoroughly, then stir in the vanilla and the orange juice.

Pour the mixture into the prepared tin and bake for about 45 minutes, until a fine skewer pushed into the middle comes out clean. Allow to cool slightly, then turn the loaf out on a wire rack to cool to room temperature.

To make the sandwiches, mix together the softened cream cheese and the bacon bits in a bowl. Cut 12 thin slices from the date loaf, and divide the cheese mixture among six of the slices, spreading it evenly. Top with the remaining six slices, press the sandwiches to enclose the filling, and cut each sandwich into two triangles.

Flapjacks

Makes 12 bars

100 g (4 oz) butter or margarine
100 g (4 oz) Demerara sugar
2 tablespoons golden syrup
225 g (8 oz) rolled oats

Preheat the oven to 180°C/350°F/gas mark 4. Grease an 18 × 25 cm (7 × 10 in) shallow baking tin. Melt the butter or margarine in a saucepan. Add the sugar and the syrup, cook for 1 minute, take off the heat and mix in the oats.

Press the mixture into the baking tin, leaving a small amount of room for expansion around the edges. Bake for about 15 to 20 minutes, until the flapjacks are golden brown. Cut into bars while still warm; take out of the tin when cold.

Store in an airtight container.

Cinnamon Toast Whirls

Makes 12 whirls

50 g (2 oz) granulated
    sugar
2 teaspoons cinnamon
12 thick slices of white
    bread, crusts removed

100 g (4 oz) butter,
    melted

Preheat the oven to 180°C/350°F/gas mark 4. Combine the sugar and cinnamon thoroughly in a bowl. Use a rolling pin to press out the bread between two pieces of greaseproof paper, rolling gently to flatten and elongate. Brush both sides of each slice with some of the melted butter, then dust one side with about 1 teaspoon of the cinnamon–sugar mixture. Roll up, starting with a long side, cinnamon side innermost. Secure the roll with a toothpick and trim both ends on the diagonal, so that the filling is exposed in a whirl pattern.

When all 12 are rolled up, place them, seam-side down, on a baking sheet, and bake for about 15 minutes, or until golden. Transfer to a wire rack and allow to cool.

Glazed Ginger Shortbread

Makes about 24 biscuits

For the shortbread
225 g (8 oz) plain white
    flour
100 g (4 oz) fine
    semolina
1 teaspoon powdered
    ginger
100 g (4 oz) caster sugar
225 g (8 oz) salted butter,
    at room temperature,
    cut into small pieces

For the topping
100 g (4 oz) butter, cut
    into small pieces
225 g (8 oz) icing sugar
1 teaspoon powdered
    ginger
2 tablespoons golden
    syrup

Preheat the oven to 150°C/300°F/gas mark 2. Lightly butter a 25 × 35 cm (11 × 14 in) baking tray. Sift the flour, the semolina and the ginger into a bowl, stir in the sugar, and add the little pieces of butter. With your hands, work the mixture to a firm dough. Put the dough into the baking tray, and press and roll it out to a depth of about 8 mm (⅓ in). Prick it all over with a fork, to stop it rising in the oven. Bake for about 40 minutes, till it is golden. Take the shortbread from the oven but leave it in the tray.

While the shortbread is cooling a little, make the topping. Put the butter in a small saucepan and sift in the icing sugar and the ginger. Heat gently, stirring, to melt the butter. Stir in the golden syrup and take the pan off the heat. Spread the glaze over the shortbread while both are still warm. When the topping has cooled just enough to set, cut the shortbread into fingers. Leave the biscuits in the tray to finish cooling, then transfer them to an airtight tin.

Petits Fours

Makes about 30 little biscuits

100 g (4 oz) soft margarine
¼ teaspoon vanilla
    essence

25 g (1 oz) icing sugar
150 g (5 oz) plain flour

Preheat the oven to 160°C/325°F/gas mark 3. Line a baking sheet with non-stick baking parchment. Put the margarine and the vanilla essence into a bowl, sift in the icing sugar, and beat to a light, fluffy cream. Work in the flour to make a stiff paste. Using a piping bag fitted with a star nozzle, pipe small stars or fingers on the baking sheet. Bake for 7 to 10 minutes, until the biscuits are dry but still pale in colour. Allow them to cool for a moment or two on the baking sheet, then transfer them to a wire rack to continue cooling.

Iced Rosehip and Redcurrant Tea

Makes about 12 glasses

6 rosehip tea bags
2 litres (3½ pints) water

250 ml (8 fl oz) syrop or
    crème de cassis
1 teaspoon lime cordial

Put the tea bags into a large teapot or heatproof jug. Bring the water to the boil, and pour it over. Leave the tea bags to steep for about 10 minutes, stirring occasionally.

Discard the bags, add the *cassis* and the lime cordial and allow the tea to cool to room temperature. Then pour it into a large plastic container. Place in the freezer. Freeze for 3 to 4 hours, until the tea is slushy. Break it up with a fork, scrape into a couple of large vacuum flasks with wide mouths, and take to the picnic.

Social Graces

Eating and drinking, as Wilkie Collins contends,
bring out the social virtues in a man.
And 'Never was the right man more entirely in the right place
than Pedgift Junior at the picnic.'

How inestimably important in its moral results – and therefore how praise-worthy in itself – is the act of eating and drinking! The social virtues centre in the stomach. A man who is not a better husband, father, and brother, after dinner than before is, digestively speaking, an incurably vicious man. What hidden charms of character disclose themselves, what dormant amiabilities awaken when our common humanity gathers together to pour out the gastric juice! . . . Now did Pedgift Junior shine brighter than ever he had shone yet, in gems of caustic humour and exquisite fertilities of resource. . . .

The last mellow hour of the day and the first cool breezes of the long summer evening had met, before the dishes were all laid waste, and the bottles as empty as bottles should be. This point in the proceedings attained, the picnic party looked lazily at Pedgift Junior to know what was to be done next. That inexhaustible functionary was equal as ever to all the calls on him. He had a new amusement ready before the quickest of the company could so much as ask him what the amusement was to be.

'Fond of music on the water, Miss Milroy?' he asked in his airiest and pleasantest manner.

Miss Milroy adored music, both on the water and the land. . .

'We'll get out of the reeds first,' said young Pedgift. He gave his orders to the boatmen – dived briskly into the little cabin – and reappeared with a concertina in his hand.

'Neat, Miss Milroy, isn't it?' he observed, pointing to his initials, inlaid on the instrument in mother-of-pearl.

WILKIE COLLINS *Armadale* 1866

Social Graces

A refined and yet exotic picnic, that will surely bring out the social graces. Like Pedgift Junior, you may feel that musical accompaniment is required!

Melon and Tomato Gazpacho

Serves 6 to 8

2 large cantaloupe or charentais melons, peeled and chopped
6 large tomatoes, peeled, seeded and chopped
1 large cucumber, peeled and seeded

1 tablespoon orange rind
8 basil leaves, finely shredded
250 ml (8 fl oz) crème fraîche, or double cream soured with the juice of 1 lemon

Put the melon and tomato pieces in the bowl of a blender or food processor. Chop two-thirds of the cucumber (reserving one-third of it unchopped), and add the pieces to the mixture in the blender or food processor. Process until velvety smooth.

Pour the soup into a bowl and stir in the orange rind and most of the basil leaves. Gently beat in the *crème fraîche* or the cream soured with lemon. When the mixture is thoroughly combined, chill for at least 2 hours, covered, in the fridge. Then pour it into a vacuum flask to take to the picnic. Chop the remaining one-third cucumber finely, and pack it, with the rest of the shredded basil, in a small container.

Serve the chilled gazpacho, topped with the cucumber and basil garnish, in sherbet glasses.

Exotic Coleslaw

Serves 6

For the dressing
50 g (2 oz) tofu, rinsed, drained and crumbled
125 ml (4 fl oz) Greek-style yogurt
1 tablespoon tahini paste
1 tablespoon Oriental sesame oil
2 teaspoons grated fresh ginger root
2 spring onions, finely chopped
2 tablespoons lemon juice
1 teaspoon soy sauce
1 teaspoon honey

For the salad
50 g (2 oz) blanched slivered almonds, toasted
900 g (2 lb) Chinese leaves, large stalks removed, finely shredded
225 g (8 oz) white radish (daikon), peeled and finely shredded
1 bunch of spring onions, trimmed and finely chopped
175 g (6 oz) mange-tout peas, trimmed and cut into thin diagonals

In a blender or food processor, combine all the ingredients for the dressing. Blend till smooth, scrape into a bowl, cover and chill.

In a large bowl, combine all the salad ingredients. Pour over the dressing, and toss to combine thoroughly. Let it sit for at least 2 hours to allow flavours to combine. If you need to keep it longer, cover and chill until needed. Pack into a large plastic bowl or box to transport.

Lobster Tart

Serves 6

For the pastry	For the filling
275 g (10 oz) plain white flour	225 g (8 oz) lobster meat, or white crab meat, flaked
A large pinch of salt	250 ml (8 fl oz) double cream
150 g (5 oz) butter and margarine, mixed	2 eggs and 1 egg yolk, beaten
A little iced water	¼ teaspoon cayenne pepper
	3 tablespoons herb cream cheese
	3 spring onions, trimmed and finely chopped
	Salt and pepper

Put the flour into a bowl, add a pinch of salt, and cut in the butter and margarine. Continue to cut, and then blend with the fingertips, until the mixture is like coarse breadcrumbs. Sprinkle in enough iced water to make the dough cohere. Take the dough from the bowl a quarter at a time, place it on a floured board, and push it away from you, using the heel of your hand. Take all the dough up and form it into a ball. Wrap it in plastic film and allow to rest in the fridge for at least 3 hours.

Preheat the oven to 190°C/375°F/gas mark 5. Grease a 20 cm (8 in) tart tin. Unwrap the pastry ball, pound it in various directions with your rolling pin, and then roll it out to a large circle. Use it to line the prepared tin.

Sprinkle the flaked shellfish over the bottom of the tart. In a bowl, beat together the cream, eggs and egg yolk, cayenne, cheese and spring onions. Add salt and pepper to taste. Pour the mixture over the shellfish. Bake in the oven for about 45 minutes, till the tart is set and golden. Allow to cool in the tart tin, and take it to the picnic in its tin.

Apricot and Almond Pudding

Serves 6

100 g (4 oz) soft margarine	100 g (4 oz) dried apricots, soaked and simmered until tender, and drained
100 g (4 oz) brown sugar	Almond essence
2 eggs	
50 g (2 oz) wholemeal flour	
100 g (4 oz) ground almonds	

Preheat the oven to 200°C/400°F/gas mark 5. Grease and flour a 20 cm (8 in) round spring-form or loose-bottomed tin. Cream together the margarine and the sugar, and beat in the eggs. Gradually work in the flour and the ground almonds, and beat the mixture with an electric mixer or by hand until it is fluffy. Pour half the batter into the tin; cover with the apricots; then pour over the remainder of the batter. Bake for about 60 minutes, till risen and golden. Allow to cool somewhat before removing from the tin; then transfer to a wire rack to finish cooling.

Spiced Cherries

I owe thanks to Margaret Costa for this recipe.

Makes 6 to 8 small jars

2.75 kg (6 lb) cherries	5 cm (2 in) stick cinnamon
4 cloves	450 g (1 lb) caster sugar
2.5 cm (1 in) piece fresh ginger root, peeled and bruised	600 ml (1 pint) white wine vinegar

Wash the cherries and prick each one once or twice with a needle. Place the spices in a muslin bag. Put the sugar and vinegar into a saucepan over a medium heat and slowly dissolve the sugar. As it begins to dissolve, add the bag of spices. Let the syrup simmer for 20 minutes, then pour it over the fruit in a large bowl. Leave the fruit to macerate for 24 hours.

Drain off the syrup from the cherries into a saucepan, warm for 20 minutes over medium heat, then pour over the cherries and leave for another 24 hours. Finally, drain off the syrup again into a saucepan, and bring to a rolling boil. Pack the cherries in sterilized jars and pour the boiling syrup over. (Be sure to remove the spices.) Leave for a few weeks before using.

An Elegant Party

Picnics were a fashionable entertainment in Jane Austen's time. Mrs Elton is determined to organize an alfresco strawberry tea. Mr Knightley's views are somewhat different.

'It is to be a morning scheme, you know, Knightley; quite a simple thing. I shall wear a large bonnet, and bring one of my little baskets hanging on my arm. Here, – probably this basket with pink ribbon. Nothing can be more simple, you see. And Jane will have such another. There is to be no form or parade – a sort of gipsy party. – We are to walk about your gardens, and gather the strawberries ourselves, and sit under trees; – and whatever else you may like to provide, it is to be all out of doors – a table spread in the shade, you know. Every thing as natural and simple as possible. Is that not your idea?'

'Not quite. My idea of the simple and the natural will be to have the table spread in the dining-room. The nature and the simplicity of gentlemen and ladies, with their servants and furniture, I think is best observed by meals within doors. When you are tired of eating strawberries in the garden, there shall be cold meat in the house.'

. . . The whole party were assembled, excepting Frank Churchill, who was expected every moment from Richmond; and Mrs Elton, in all her apparatus of happiness, her large bonnet and her basket, was very ready to lead the way in gathering, accepting, or talking – strawberries, and only strawberries, could now be thought or spoken of. – The best fruit in England – every body's favourite – always wholesome. – These the finest beds and finest sorts. – Delightful to gather for one's self – the only way of really enjoying them. – Morning decidedly the best time – never tired – every sort good – hautboy infinitely superior – no comparison – the others hardly eatable – hautboys very scarce – Chili preferred – white wood finest flavour of all – price of strawberries in London – abundance about Bristol – Maple Grove – cultivation – beds when to be renewed – gardeners thinking exactly different – no general rule – gardeners never to be put out of their way – delicious fruit – only too rich to be eaten much of – inferior to cherries – currants more refreshing – only objection to gathering strawberries the stooping – glaring sun – tired to death – could bear it no longer – must go and sit in the shade.'

JANE AUSTEN *Emma* 1816

An Elegant Party

Celery hearts and salmon in pastry – here rendered as the Russian koulibiac – are classic dishes that have survived from a more gracious era. Strawberries in rose cream complete the picture of sylvan elegance.

Celery Hearts Casino

Serves 6

3 heads celery, trimmed of
  outer stalks and top
1 can of chicken
  consommé
350 ml (12 fl oz)
  vinaigrette dressing
  (see page 25)
½ teaspoon paprika
A dash of cayenne pepper
200 ml (7 fl oz) double
  cream
2 large eggs, hard-boiled
  and finely chopped
1½ tablespoons finely
  chopped parsley

Cut the celery hearts in half lengthwise. Put them in a large casserole, spoon in the chicken consommé and add enough water to cover the celery. Slowly bring the stock to the boil, then reduce the heat and simmer for 10 minutes. Remove from the heat and allow to stand for a further 5 minutes. Lift the celery hearts out with a slotted spoon, and reserve the stock for another use.

Arrange the celery hearts in two shallow dishes, three to a dish. Pour over the vinaigrette dressing and leave to marinate, turning occasionally, for at least 3 hours.

Remove the celery hearts from the marinade. Pour the vinaigrette into a jug, stir in the paprika and cayenne, then beat in the cream slowly. Pour into a bottle to transport.

Pack the celery hearts into a plastic box, in two layers if necessary, and cover. Mix the chopped hard-boiled eggs with the parsley. Pack into a small jar.

To serve, help each person to a celery heart. Give the cream vinaigrette a shake and pour some over each celery heart. Scatter with the chopped egg and parsley garnish.

Koulibiac

Serves 6 to 8

450 g (1 lb) frozen puff
  pastry
100 g (4 oz) long-grain
  rice
Chicken stock (optional)
100 g (4 oz) unsalted
  butter
6 spring onions, finely
  chopped
100 g (4 oz) mushrooms,
  sliced
450 g (1 lb) salmon, in
  two trimmed and
  skinned fillets, each
  about 2.5 cm (1 in)
  thick
1 glass of dry white wine
1 teaspoon fresh parsley
1 teaspoon chopped fresh
  tarragon
Salt and pepper
4 eggs, 3 hard-boiled,
  1 beaten
Soured cream

The day, or at least several hours, before you intend to make the *koulibiac*, take the pastry from the freezer and leave it to come to room temperature.

If chicken stock is available, cook the rice in it – if not, seasoned water will do. When the rice is cooked, allow it to cool.

In a frying pan, melt half of the butter and sauté the spring onions and the mushrooms. Remove the vegetables from the pan and reserve them. Melt the rest of the butter, add the fish, pour over the white wine, cover, and simmer for 10 minutes. Drain and flake the fish. In a large bowl, mix together the rice, the salmon and the mushrooms and onion. Stir in the parsley and tarragon and season to taste. Cut the hard-boiled eggs into quarters.

Grease a baking sheet. Divide the pastry into two and roll each part into a long rectangle. Place one on the prepared baking sheet and spoon half the filling down the centre, to within 2.5 cm (1 in) of the edges. Distribute the egg quarters on the filling, and cover with the remaining salmon mixture. Dampen the edges of the pastry with water, then cover the filling with the second pastry oblong. Slash the top of the pastry with diagonal vents at 2.5 (1 in) intervals. Allow the pastry to rest for 30 minutes.

Meanwhile, preheat the oven to 220°C/425°F/gas mark 7. Bake the *koulibiac* for about 30 minutes, until the pastry is golden. Allow to cool to room temperature.

Pack soured cream in a covered bowl to take to the picnic, and serve it as an accompaniment.

Summer Vegetables in Sesame Dressing

Serves 6

For the salad
225 g (8 oz) asparagus,
    trimmed and cut into
    4 cm (1½ in) slices
100 g (4 oz) mange-tout
    peas, trimmed
100 g (4 oz) French
    beans, topped and
    tailed
675 g (1½ lb) cauliflower
    florets
675 g (1½ lb) broccoli
    florets
225 g (8 oz) courgettes,
    trimmed and sliced into
    rounds
450 g (1 lb) new potatoes

For the dressing
225 g (8 oz) curd cheese
60 ml (2 fl oz) sesame oil
1 small clove of garlic,
    crushed
1 tablespoon lemon juice
A large handful of
    coriander, trimmed
    from the stalks
A dash of red pepper flakes
125 ml (4 fl oz) single
    cream
2 tablespoons sesame
    seeds, lightly toasted

Bring a large saucepan of water to the boil. Drop in the asparagus, and cook for about 3 minutes, or until just tender. Remove with a slotted spoon, refresh under running cold water, and reserve in a large bowl. Drop the mange-tout peas into the boiling water for half a minute, refresh and reserve in the bowl with the asparagus. Cook the French beans for 2 minutes, then refresh and reserve with the other vegetables. Cook the cauliflower and broccoli together for 3 minutes, refresh and add to the vegetable collection in the bowl. Cook the courgettes for 2 minutes, refresh and add to the bowl. Finally cook the new potatoes for 10 to 15 minutes, refresh, cut in half, and add to the bowl.

Use a blender or food processor to make the dressing. Combine all the ingredients except the cream and the sesame seeds, and blend until they are broken down and well combined. Gradually blend in the cream. Scrape the dressing into a bowl and stir in the toasted sesame seeds.

Pour the dressing over the blanched vegetables and toss gently to coat evenly. Pack the salad in a plastic box to take to the picnic.

Strawberries with Rose Cream

The recipe is given in Margaret Costa's *Four Seasons Cookery Book*.

Serves 6

450 g (1 lb) strawberries,
    hulled
2 tablespoons kirsch
5 tablespoons vanilla
    sugar

2 eggs, separated
150 ml (¼ pint) milk
300 ml (½ pint) double
    cream
3 drops of rose water

Arrange the strawberries in the bottom half of a china bowl. Sprinkle over them 1 tablespoon of the kirsch and 3 tablespoons of the sugar.

Make the custard. Put the egg yolks into a bowl, with 1 tablespoon of the sugar, and beat well. Pour the milk into a saucepan and just bring to the boil. Stirring all the time, pour the hot milk over the egg mixture. Return the mixture to the saucepan and heat gently, still stirring, till the custard thickens. Take from the heat and stir in the rest of the kirsch.

Beat the egg whites with the remaining tablespoon of sugar. Whip the cream with the rose water, and gently fold in first the egg whites, then, little by little, the custard. Pile the rose cream on top of the strawberries. Chill.

Cover the top of the bowl with plastic film – and carry it with great care.

Picnic Fruits

In A Midsummer Night's Dream *love-smitten Titania feeds Bottom*
'with apricocks and dewberries, with purple grapes, green figs, and mulberries'.
Fruit is the perfect picnic food:
fresh, delicious, conveniently packaged and easy to transport.

A yellow-coated pomegranate, figs like lizard's necks,
    a handful of half-rosy part-ripe grapes,
a quince all delicate-downed and fragrant fleeced,
    a walnut winking out from its green shell,
a cucumber with the bloom on it pouting from its leaf-bed,
    and a ripe gold-coated olive –

PHILIP OF THESSALONIKA *c.* A.D. 40, trans. Edwin Morgan
in Peter Jay *The Greek Anthology* 1973

The proper way to eat a fig, in society,
Is to split it in four, holding it by the stump,
And open it, so that it is a glittering, rosy, moist, honied,
    heavy-petalled four-petalled flower.

Then you throw away the skin
Which is just like a four-sepalled calyx,
After you have taken off the blossom with your lips.

But the vulgar way
Is just to put your mouth to the crack, and take out the
    flesh in one bite.

D.H. LAWRENCE 'Figs' 1920–23

Picnic Fruits

This picnic has fruit, fresh or dried, in every course, but, because of the contrasting textures and flavours, each is fresh and delightful, with no sense of repetition or excess.

Avocado Caribbean

Serves 6

3 large ripe avocados
6 small limes

1 miniature bottle of rum
Salt and pepper

Bring the separate ingredients to the picnic. To serve, slice each avocado in half and remove the stone. Put a drop or two of rum in the centre of each avocado, and squeeze the juice of 1 lime over the surface and into the centre hole to mix with the rum. Season to taste with the salt and pepper.

Melon and Sesame Surprise

Serves 6

3 medium charantais or
   canteloupe melons,
   peeled, seeded and cut
   into chunks
60 ml (2 fl oz) fresh
   lemon juice

3 tablespoons sugar
1 tablespoon sesame seeds,
   lightly toasted
Pepper to taste

In a large bowl, toss the melon chunks with the lemon juice and 2 tablespoons of the sugar. Chop and bruise the sesame seeds to release their pungent flavour, then combine them with the remaining sugar and the pepper in a small bowl. Sprinkle half the sesame mixture over the melon and toss again. Spoon the mixture into a plastic bowl or box and sprinkle the rest of the sesame mixture over the top. Chill.

Duck Salad with Two Fruits

If blueberries are available, try substituting them for the raspberries – their taste goes wonderfully well with the duck. If you can get hold of blueberry vinegar (or make your own by pricking blueberries and leaving them for a week in white wine vinegar, then straining), so much the better.

Serves 6

3 wild ducks, trimmed of
   excess skin and fat and
   cleaned
Salt and pepper
4 tablespoons raspberry
   vinegar
2 teaspoons French
   mustard
2 tablespoons crème de
   cassis
3 tablespoons fresh lemon
   juice

150 ml (¼ pint)
   sunflower oil
12 leaves of radicchio
2 oranges, carefully
   trimmed of pith, cut
   into rounds
100 g (4 oz) fresh
   raspberries
5 sprigs of mint, stalks
   removed, trimmed and
   chopped into thin
   ribbons

Preheat the oven to 230°C/450°F/gas mark 8. Dry the ducks, prick them all over, rub with salt and pepper and place them on a roasting rack over a pan. Roast for 20 minutes in the hot oven, then reduce the heat to 150°C/300°F/gas mark 2 and cook for 1½ hours more. Let the ducks cool, then chill them overnight. You should be able to pull the skin off easily. Reserve the skin. Remove the meat from the bones and chop it into bite-sized pieces.

Scrape and clean off any excess fat from the skin, place it in a single layer in a baking tray, salt it lightly, and cook in a moderate oven, 180°C/350°F/gas mark 4, for

about 15 minutes, until the skin is crisp. Remove the crackling from the oven, pat it dry, and allow it to continue drying in the open air. Then tear and crumble it into pieces as small as possible.

Make the dressing: beat together the vinegar, mustard, *crème de cassis*, lemon juice and seasoning. Add the oil in a thin stream, continuously beating until the dressing is completely emulsified. Bottle it to take to the picnic separately.

Line a portable container with the radicchio leaves. Spoon in some of the duck meat and crackling, sprinkle with a few orange slices and raspberries and a little chopped mint. Cover the salad. Before serving, shake the dressing in its bottle, pour over the salad and toss gently to avoid damaging the fruit.

Salad Elona

Serves 6

1 cucumber, peeled and   *Salt and pepper*
   very thinly sliced   *2 tablespoons champagne*
450 g (1 lb) strawberries,   *or white wine vinegar*
   hulled and halved

In a shallow round or oval serving dish or porcelain quiche dish, arrange the sliced cucumber and the halved strawberries in overlapping concentric circles, the strawberries arranged with the cut sides facing up in one circle and down in the next, divided by a circle of cucumber slices.

When you have completed the arrangement and topped it with a decorative fan of strawberries, sprinkle over the vinegar. Cover the salad with plastic film and transport to the picnic.

Figs and Cheese

Serves 6

150 g (5 oz) cream cheese   *About 18 figs, fresh if*
A small fresh goat's cheese   *available, otherwise*
                                  dried

Mash together the cream cheese and the goat's cheese in a bowl. If fresh figs are in season, bring them to the picnic whole, and pack the cheese mixture separately in a small decorative bowl. Pass the cheese with a small knife, so that people can help themselves to a little to accompany the fruit. If you are using dried figs, slit the fruit and insert a little of the cheese mixture as a filling. Pack the stuffed fruit in a plastic box.

A Lakeside Fantasy

*The sisters Ursula and Gudrun snatch a moment of perfect
happiness at a water-party which is to end in tragedy.
Place, time and mood blend to enchantment.*

. . . they lifted their boat on to the bank and looked round with joy. They
were quite alone in a forsaken little stream-mouth, and on the knoll just
behind was a clump of trees.

'We will bathe just for a moment,' said Ursula, 'and then we'll have tea.'
In less than a minute Ursula had thrown off her clothes and had slipped naked
into the water, and was swimming out. Quickly, Gudrun joined her. They
swam silently and blissfully for a few minutes, circling round their little
stream-mouth. Then they slipped ashore and ran into the grove again, like
nymphs.

'How lovely it is to be free,' said Ursula, running swiftly here and there
between the tree trunks, quite naked, her hair blowing loose. . . .

When they had run and danced themselves dry, the girls quickly dressed
and sat down to the fragrant tea. They sat on the northern side of the grove, in
the yellow sunshine, facing the slope of the grassy hill, alone in a little wild
world of their own. The tea was hot and aromatic, there were delicious little
sandwiches of cucumber and of caviare, and winy cakes.

'Are you happy, Prune?' cried Ursula in delight, looking at her sister.

'Ursula, I'm perfectly happy,' replied Gudrun gravely, looking at the
westering sun.

'So am I.'

When they were together, doing the things they enjoyed, the two sisters
were quite complete in a perfect world of their own. And this was one of the
perfect moments of freedom and delight, such as children alone know, when
all seems a perfect and blissful adventure.

D.H. LAWRENCE *Women in Love* 1916

A Lakeside Fantasy

*Imagination is the prime requirement of the picnic chef: a bit of
culinary daring can pay dividends.*

Profiteroles with Tomato Cream and Chicken Mousse

Makes 20 profiteroles

For the tomato cream
175 g (6 oz) curd cheese
3 tablespoons dried
   tomatoes packed in oil,
   drained and chopped
Freshly ground black
   pepper
4 tablespoons double
   cream, whipped

For the chicken mousse
1 large chicken breast,
   cooked and chopped
4 sprigs of tarragon,
   trimmed and finely
   chopped
Salt

Freshly ground black
   pepper
Cayenne pepper
150 ml (¼ pint) aspic
3 tablespoons double
   cream
2 egg whites, softly
   whipped

For the profiteroles
50 g (2 oz) unsalted
   butter
4 tablespoons milk
4 tablespoons water
65 g (2½ oz) flour
A pinch of salt
2 eggs, beaten

Make the fillings first. For the tomato cream, put the
curd cheese and the dried tomatoes in a bowl and
season with the pepper. Beat until thoroughly
combined, then fold in the whipped cream.

Use a food processor to make the chicken mousse. Put
the chicken and tarragon in the processor, season with
salt, black pepper, and cayenne, and process till smooth.
Scrape into a bowl and stir in the cooled, but not set,
aspic. Fold in the double cream and leave to thicken.
Then fold in the beaten egg whites. Chill in the fridge
till set.

Now make the profiteroles. Preheat the oven to 200°C/
400°F/gas mark 6, and lightly grease a baking sheet. Melt
the butter in a heavy saucepan set over a low heat. Add
the milk and water and bring to the boil. Immediately
remove from the heat and pour in the flour and salt.
Beat until the flour has absorbed all the liquid, and the
dough comes away from the sides of the pan. Cool
slightly, then gradually beat in the eggs. The dough
should be shiny and thick.

Using a piping bag fitted with a plain nozzle, pipe the
choux pastry into 20 small bun shapes. Bake for about
20 minutes, until they are puffed, golden and crisp.
Remove and cool on a wire rack.

When the puffs are cool, split them, but not quite all the
way through. Fill the hollow centres with the two
stuffing mixtures – 10 with the tomato cream and 10
with the chicken mousse. Pack into plastic boxes to take
to the picnic.

Cracked Wheat Salad

Serves 6

350 g (12 oz) cracked
   wheat or bulgur
2 teaspoons salt
3 tablespoons lemon juice
2 tablespoons olive oil
½ teaspoon chopped
   garlic
75 g (3 oz) chopped walnuts

50 g (2 oz) currants
3 tablespoons finely
   chopped spring onion
4 tablespoons finely
   chopped parsley
3 tomatoes, finely chopped
1 orange, grated rind
Pepper

Soak the cracked wheat in boiling water to cover for 1 hour; stir in the salt. Drain thoroughly and pat dry with paper towels.

Now toss the wheat with the lemon juice and olive oil and let it marinate, covered, in the fridge for 4 hours. Then add the remaining ingredients, season with pepper, toss the salad well, and pack into a plastic bowl or box to take to the picnic.

Smoked Salmon Tartlets

Makes 6 tartlets

For the pastry
100 g (4 oz) plain flour
50 g (2 oz) butter
1 egg yolk
A dash of water

For the filling
100 g (4 oz) smoked
  salmon pieces, finely
  chopped
3 tablespoons sliced spring
  onions
2 eggs
6 tablespoons single
  cream
Tabasco
Worcestershire sauce
1 teaspoon lemon juice
Salt and pepper

Grease 6 × 7.5 cm (3 in) tartlet tins. To make the pastry, rub together the flour and the butter until the mixture resembles fine breadcrumbs. Then add the egg yolk and work with the hands until you have a moderately soft dough – add a tiny bit of water if necessary. Knead lightly, roll out, and use to line the tartlet tins. Prick the bases with a fork.

Preheat the oven to 190°C/375°F/gas mark 5. Arrange the chopped salmon on the bases of the tartlet shells and sprinkle over some of the sliced spring onion.

Beat together the eggs and cream, add drops of the Tabasco and Worcestershire sauce to taste, and stir in the lemon juice, salt and pepper. Pour some of the mixture into each tartlet. Bake for about 35 minutes, until the filling is puffed and golden. Allow to cool, then pack into an airtight container.

Port wine cakes

Makes 6 to 8 slices

1 plain madeira cake
12 lumps of sugar
2 medium oranges
450 ml (¾ pint) port and
  water mixed

2 sticks of cinnamon
3 sprigs of tarragon
1 tablespoon gelatine

Cut the madeira cake into thin slices and use to line the bottom of an 18 × 25 cm (7 × 10 in) baking tray. Rub the sugar lumps over the oranges to absorb as much orange oil as possible. Place the sugar in a small saucepan, together with the mixed port and water, cinnamon, tarragon and gelatine. Heat very carefully until the sugar and the gelatine are dissolved. Do not let the mixture boil. Remove it from the heat and allow to cool for one hour. Stir again and strain over the cake slices. Chill in the fridge until set, then slice into 6 to 8 portions.

Pack in a plastic box to transport; keep cool.

Strawberry Whip

Serves 6

50 g (2 oz) caster sugar
3 eggs separated
450 ml (¾ pint) double
  cream

450 g (1 lb) fresh
  strawberries, hulled and
  chopped

Whisk the caster sugar and the egg yolks in a heatproof bowl until they are well combined. Then place the bowl in a saucepan and fill the pan with boiling water to half-way up the sides of the bowl (or, alternatively, use a double boiler). Set the pan on a low heat and cook the mixture, whisking, until it is thick enough to ribbon when the whisk is lifted. Take off the heat and allow to cool.

Whisk the egg whites until they form soft peaks. In another bowl, whip the cream until thick. Stir the chopped strawberries into the egg yolk mixture, then fold in the whipped cream. Finally, fold in the whisked egg whites, very gently. Turn the whip into 6 individual glasses or 1 large bowl. Chill for several hours or overnight.

To transport, cover the glasses or bowl with plastic film. Keep upright.

Bottled Sunshine

*The Water Rat is fascinated by the raffish Sea Rat, with his tales
of the warm South. The Sea Rat's hint that
'sometimes I dream of the shellfish of Marseilles, and wake up crying!'
prompts courteous Ratty to offer him lunch.*

'That reminds me,' said the polite Water Rat; 'you happened to mention that
you were hungry, and I ought to have spoken earlier. Of course you will stop
and take your midday meal with me? My hole is close by; it is some time past
noon, and you are very welcome to whatever there is.'

'Now I call that kind and brotherly of you,' said the Sea Rat. 'I was indeed
hungry when I sat down, and ever since I inadvertently happened to mention
shellfish my pangs have been extreme. But couldn't you fetch it along out
here? I am none too fond of going under hatches, unless I'm obliged to . . .'

'That is indeed an excellent suggestion,' said the Water Rat, and hurried off
home. There he got out the luncheon-basket and packed a simple meal, in
which, remembering the stranger's origin and preferences, he took care to
include a yard of long French bread, a sausage out of which the garlic sang,
some cheese which lay down and cried, and a long-necked straw-covered
flask containing bottled sunshine shed and garnered on far Southern slopes.
Thus laden, he returned with all speed, and blushed for pleasure at the old
seaman's commendations of his taste and judgement, as together they
unpacked the basket and laid out the contents on the grass by the roadside.

KENNETH GRAHAME *The Wind in the Willows* 1908

Bottled Sunshine

The flavours of the cuisines of the sun
dapple this picnic.

Summer Dolmades

These dolmades are ersatz (lettuce leaves for vine leaves, crab for lamb), but none the less delicious.

Makes 12 dolmades

12 large lettuce leaves (cos or Iceberg)	350 g (12 oz) white crab meat, flaked
5 spring onions chopped	1 teaspoon chopped parsley
100 g (4 oz) long-grained rice	1 teaspoon chopped dill
75 g (3 oz) butter	Salt and pepper
600 ml (1 pint) fish stock	½ lemon, strained juice

Blanch the lettuce leaves by plunging them in boiling water for 1 or 2 minutes. Drain. Sauté the onions and the rice in the butter until just translucent, then add enough of the stock to cover the rice. Put on a lid and cook the rice until the liquid is absorbed and the rice is tender. Let the rice cool slightly and mix with the crab meat and herbs. Season with salt and pepper.

Preheat the oven to 160°C/325°F/gas mark 3. Spread out the lettuce leaves and put a spoonful of filling on each. Fold the long edges of the leaves over and roll up into neat parcels. Pack the dolmades in a baking dish just large enough to hold them, pour over the remaining stock (with a little extra water, if needed), and sprinkle over the lemon juice.

Cover and bake for 1 hour. Let the dolmades cool in the liquid, then lift them out with a slotted spoon and pack in a plastic box for the picnic.

Chicken and Vegetable Aïoli

Serves 6

For the aïoli

10 cloves of garlic, peeled and chopped	2 red peppers, seeded and thinly sliced
2 egg yolks, at room temperature	2 green peppers, seeded and thinly sliced
Salt and pepper	6 medium carrots, peeled, trimmed and sliced into fingers
1½ teaspoons Dijon mustard	225 g (8 oz) green beans, trimmed, blanched and refreshed
1 lemon, strained juice	
350 ml (12 fl oz) olive oil and sunflower oil, mixed half and half	1 large cauliflower, cut into florets, blanched and refreshed
6 large sprigs of parsley	225 g (8 oz) button mushrooms, wiped clean

For the salad

12 chicken drumsticks, browned, baked and chilled	12 spring onions, trimmed
	30 black olives
18 large prawns, cooked	4 courgettes, trimmed, blanched and cut into fingers
6 globe artichokes, trimmed, boiled until tender, choke removed	
	675 g (1½ lb) small new potatoes, boiled in their jackets
6 large sprigs of parsley	
225 g (8 oz) cherry tomatoes, washed	6 hard-boiled eggs, shelled and quartered

Aïoli is traditionally prepared using a mortar and pestle. But a blender or food processor makes the job much easier. Put the garlic, egg yolks, salt and pepper, mustard and lemon juice in a blender or food processor. Blend until smooth. Then slowly pour in the oil, and continue to blend until the sauce is emulsified. Transfer to a bowl and cover; chill for several hours to allow the flavours to amalgamate.

Pack the cooked chicken and shellfish in separate plastic boxes. Place the artichokes and the parsley in a plastic bag, and pack all the other cut vegetables and the eggs in plastic boxes. Chill everything until you are ready to depart. Then pack all the containers, together with six large plates. To serve, put an artichoke in the centre of each plate and fill its centre with some of the *aïoli*. Stick a sprig of parsley on top. Surround the artichoke with a selection of the vegetables, 4 egg quarters, 2 chicken drumsticks and 3 prawns. Everything – chicken, prawns, egg, vegetables and artichoke leaves – is dipped into the *aïoli* before being eaten.

Herby Tomato and Cheese Flatbread

Serves up to 10

Sunflower oil
Cornmeal
5 teaspoons dried yeast
475 ml (16 fl oz)
*   lukewarm water*
675 g (1½ lb) plain white
*   flour*
2½ teaspoons sea salt
2 teaspoons dried
*   oregano*
2 teaspoons dried thyme
2 teaspoons dried dill
½ teaspoon crumbled
*   dried rosemary*

About 200 ml (7 fl oz)
*   olive oil*
350 g (12 oz) mozzarella
*   or mild provolone*
*   cheese*
675 g (1½ lb) plum or
*   beefsteak tomatoes,*
*   sliced as thinly as*
*   possible*
100 g (4 oz) black olives,
*   pitted and halved*
Parmesan cheese

Oil a heavy 30 cm (12 in) cast iron frying pan with the sunflower oil. Sprinkle the base with cornmeal. In a large bowl mix the yeast with 125 ml (4 fl oz) of the warm water and leave for 15 minutes, or until foamy. Stir in 200 g (7 oz) of the flour, and the salt, oregano, thyme, dill and rosemary; gradually add 175 ml (6 fl oz) of the olive oil and the rest of the water; combine well. Stir in another 400 g (14 oz) of the flour and form the dough into a ball. Knead on a floured board, adding as much of the remaining 75 g (3 oz) flour as necessary to make a smooth and elastic dough. Continue to work and knead for about 20 minutes, until the dough is no longer sticky. Form into a ball, place in an oiled bowl and turn to cover in the oil. Cover the bowl with plastic film and allow the dough to rise for 45 minutes to 1 hour, or until it has doubled in size.

Punch down the dough, knead it and divide it into two equal portions. Put half in the oiled pan and press down to cover the bottom well. Using your fingertips, make depressions all over the dough. Brush the dough with 1 tablespoon of olive oil and cover with half the cheese, leaving a small border all around the edges of the bread. Cover with the thin slices of tomato, overlapping them. Sprinkle the remaining salt over the tomatoes, then cover them with the rest of the cheese. Flatten the remaining dough on a surface and lay it over the filling, pressing down the edges to enclose the filling. Use the fingers to make more depressions all over the top of the dough. Arrange the pitted olives in the depressions. Brush the top of the dough with the remaining olive oil, sprinkle with a handful of Parmesan, and cover with a tea towel. Leave to rise in a warm place for half an hour. Meanwhile, preheat the oven to 200°C/400°F/gas mark 6.

Bake for about 1 hour, or until golden brown at the edges. Allow to cool somewhat before carefully removing from the pan. Wrap in foil to take to the picnic, and serve it cut into wedges.

Putting on the Style

*Only the best will do
for Tennyson's picnickers at Audley Court,
who feast from damask
in the secluded orchard.*

'The Bull, the Fleece are cramm'd, and
   not a room
For love or money. Let us picnic there
At Audley Court.'
     I spoke, while Audley feast
Humm'd like a hive all round the narrow
   quay,
To Francis, with a basket on his arm,
To Francis just alighted from the boat,
And breathing of the sea. 'With all my
   heart,'
Said Francis. Then we shoulder'd thro'
   the swarm,
And rounded by the stillness of the beach
To where the bay runs up its latest horn.
     We left the dying ebb that faintly lipp'd
The flat red granite; so by many a sweep
Of meadow smooth from aftermath we
   reach'd
The griffin-guarded gates, and pass'd thro'
   all
The pillar'd dusk of sounding sycamores,

And cross'd the garden to the gardener's
   lodge,
With all its casements bedded, and its walls
And chimneys muffled in the leafy vine.
There, on a slope of orchard, Francis laid
A damask napkin wrought with horse and
   hound,
Brought out a dusky loaf that smelt of
   home,
And, half-cut-down, a pasty costly-made,
Where quail and pigeon, lark and leveret
   lay,
Like fossils of the rock, with golden yolks
Imbedded and injellied; last, with these,
A flask of cider from his father's vats,
Prime, which I knew; and so we sat and eat
And talk'd old matters over; who was dead,
Who married, who was like to be, and how
The races went, and who would rent the
   hall. . .

ALFRED, LORD TENNYSON 'Audley Court' 1838

Putting on the Style

Tuck these superior morsels into your hamper, pack the silver and porcelain, and bring the candelabra and an ice bucket for the champagne – this movable feast will draw envious glances from other outdoor revellers.

Quails' Eggs and Vegetables with Tapenade

Serves about 6

16 quail's eggs	For the tapenade
½ small cauliflower	50 g (2 oz) black olives
1 head of endive	3 anchovy fillets
6 carrots	1 clove of garlic, chopped
1 small cucumber	2 tablespoons capers
6 stalks of celery	3 tablespoons tinned
8 to 12 radishes	tuna, drained
8 to 12 spring onions	1 teaspoon lemon juice
12 to 16 cherry tomatoes	A small handful of basil
	leaves, stalks removed
	A small handful of parsley,
	stalks removed
	60 ml (2 fl oz) olive oil
	60 ml (2 fl oz)
	mayonnaise

To boil the quail's eggs, place them in a single layer in a saucepan. Cover them with cold water, and bring them just to the boil; turn down the heat and simmer for 6 minutes. Pour off the hot water, cover with cold water, and leave the eggs till they are cool enough to handle. You may peel the eggs and wrap them in plastic to take to the picnic, or leave them in their shells and let everyone peel their own.

Prepare the vegetables. Divide the cauliflower into 12 to 16 florets and the endive into leaves; peel and trim the carrots and cut them into fingers; cut the cucumber into fingers; trim and halve the celery stalks; trim the radishes and the spring onions; leave the cherry tomatoes whole, with their stalks.

To make the *tapenade,* put all the ingredients except the olive oil and the mayonnaise into a blender or food processor, and blend to a smooth paste. Slowly blend in the oil, and then the mayonnaise. The dip should have a light, clinging consistency.

To transport, pack the quail's eggs and the prepared vegetables into plastic boxes. Pour the dip into a decorative bowl and cover it with plastic film.

To serve, offer everyone a selection of vegetables and some of the quail's eggs to put on their plates. People may put a little of the dip on their plates, or reach into the communal bowl, as they prefer.

Jellied Pigeon with Cherries

This recipe is a simplified version of one given by Elizabeth David in an article written many years ago.

Serves 6

3 pigeons, cleaned	3 stalks of celery, with
Salt and pepper	leaves, chopped
450 g (1 lb) cherries	3 sprigs of parsley,
A glass of kirsch	trimmed and chopped
1 calf's foot	1 bay leaf, crumbled
1 carrot, trimmed and	½ tablespoon chopped
sliced	fresh thyme

Preheat the oven to 160°C/325°F/gas mark 3. Season the pigeons inside and out. Stone the cherries, pour the kirsch over them and leave them to macerate. Put the pigeons, together with the calf's foot and the vegetables and herbs, into a large casserole. Pour over enough water almost to cover. Put the lid on the casserole, place it in the oven and cook for about 2 hours, or until the juices run clear when the pigeons' breasts are pierced. Allow the pigeons to cool in the casserole.

When the birds are cool enough to handle, take them from the casserole (leaving the cooking liquid in the casserole to continue cooling), and remove the breasts. Arrange the breasts in an attractive rimmed dish that you can take to the picnic. Cover with plastic film and chill.

When the cooking liquid has cooled enough for a layer of fat to form on the surface, skim this off. Bring the liquid to the boil on top of the cooker and boil until it is reduced by about one-third. Then leave it to cool.

Take the cherries from their marinade and arrange them around the pigeon meat. When the cooking liquid is fairly cool, but still liquid, pour it over the pigeons and the cherries in the dish. Cover and chill in the fridge for several hours, till the sauce has set in a jelly round them. It will not be as clear and colourless as a pure aspic or bought gelatine, but it will have far more flavour.

Broad Beans with Artichoke Hearts

Serves 6

450 g (1 lb) shelled broad beans (about 1.25 kg/ 2½ lb unshelled)	*1 275 g (10 oz) bottle of marinated artichoke hearts, drained and halved*
1 purple onion, finely sliced	*2 egg yolks*
	1 lemon, strained juice
	A few springs of fresh dill
	Salt and pepper

Cook the broad beans in boiling salted water for about 20 minutes, until they are tender. Drain them, and reserve 450 ml (¾ pint) of the cooking liquid. Place the drained beans in a bowl and add the onion and the artichoke hearts.

In a saucepan, beat together the reserved cooking liquid, the egg yolks and the lemon juice. Set over a low heat and continue stirring until the sauce is thickened and a little frothy. Take off the heat, stir in the dill and the salt and pepper to taste, and pour over the beans in the bowl. Allow to cool slightly, then cover and chill in the fridge for a few hours. Transfer to an easily carried container to take to the picnic.

Chocolate Truffle Mousses

Makes about 6

225 g (8 oz) plain chocolate	*2 tablespoons brandy, rum, Cointreau or Grand Marnier*
2 teaspoons instant coffee	*600 ml (1 pint) double cream*
2 tablespoons water	

Break 150 g (5 oz) of the chocolate into squares and put it with the coffee and the water into a bowl set over a pan of hot water. When the chocolate has melted, stir in the brandy, rum or orange liqueur. Allow to cool slightly.

Chop the remaining chocolate into little chips, and whip half of the cream. Fold the melted chocolate mixture and the chocolate chips into the whipped cream. Spoon the mousse into little ramekins and chill.

Shortly before you leave for the picnic, whip the remaining cream. Transfer it to a small bowl. Pack the ramekins and the bowl with the cream in a single layer in a plastic box, and cover the box. Transport in an insulated box or bag. Put a dollop of cream on top of each mousse just before serving.

An Indian Summer

In Heat and Dust *the Nawab woos Olivia*
with an invitation to 'a little picnic
somewhere in some shady spot'.

He had come with two cars, a Rolls and an Alfa Romeo. All the young men with him piled into the Alfa Romeo while he himself, Olivia, and Harry sat in the Rolls. . . . They had arrived in a shady grove around a small stone shrine. It was cool and green here; there was even the sound of water. There was also a retinue of Palace servants who had already prepared the place for their entertainment. The ground had been spread with carpets and cushions on which Olivia was invited to recline. The Nawab and Harry joined her while the young men were sent off to amuse themselves elsewhere. The servants were busy unpacking hampers and cooling bottles of wine. . . .

Now [the Nawab] was in an excellent mood and the party began to go with a swing. The servants had unpacked the picnic hampers, filling the sacred grove with roasted chickens, quails, and potted shrimps. The young men were very lively and entertained sometimes with practical jokes which they played on each other, and sometimes with songs and Urdu verses. One of them had brought a lute-like instrument out of which he plucked some bittersweet notes.

RUTH PRAWER JHABVALA *Heat and Dust* 1975

An Indian Summer

*A meal that will bring the flavours of the East to your picnic table. The
mellow clementines in their luxurious syrup provide a subtle
counterpoint to the overt spiciness of the other recipes.*

Curried Chickpeas and Limes

Serves 6

4 tablespoons sunflower oil	¾ teaspoon cayenne pepper
2 large onions, finely chopped	¾ teaspoon ground turmeric
1 green pepper, seeded and finely chopped	3 cans (about 425 g/ 15 oz) cooked chickpeas, drained and rinsed
3 cloves of garlic, crushed	
1 tablespoon minced fresh ginger	
2 large tomatoes, chopped	250 ml (8 fl oz) water
1½ teaspoons ground cumin	4 small limes
1 teaspoon celery seeds	50 g (2 oz) fresh coriander, trimmed, stalks removed, and chopped

Combine the oil, onions, pepper, garlic and ginger in a
frying pan set over a medium heat; stir, and cook until
the onions are transparent and the pepper soft. Add the
tomatoes and cook, stirring, until almost all of the liquid
evaporates. Scatter in the cumin, celery seeds, cayenne
and turmeric; stir for about 5 minutes, until the spices
are pungent and combined with the sauce. Add the
chickpeas and stir in the water.

Cover and simmer over a low heat for about 20 minutes;
if the sauce is not thick after this time, remove the lid
and continue to cook at a higher heat until it is. Squeeze
two of the limes over the chickpeas and stir the juice in.

Allow the chickpeas to cool, then spoon them into a
plastic box. Sprinkle with the chopped coriander. Cut
the remaining limes into quarters, and place them
attractively on top of the salad. Cover and chill.

Chicken Bengal

Serves 6

12 chicken legs	½ teaspoon salt
175 g (6 oz) butter, melted	1¼ teaspoons paprika
2 tablespoons curry powder	A pinch of cayenne pepper
	1¼ teaspoons yogurt
2 teaspoons mustard powder	1½ teaspoons Worcestershire sauce
4 tablespoons mango chutney	150 g (5 oz) fresh breadcrumbs

Skin all of the pieces of chicken. In a bowl, mix together
the melted butter, curry powder, mustard, chutney, salt,
paprika, cayenne, yogurt and Worcestershire sauce. Stir
until thoroughly combined.

Place the chicken pieces in a shallow dish which just
holds them. Pour the mixture over them and turn to
coat thoroughly. Allow to sit in the marinade for 3 to 4
hours.

Preheat the grill of the cooker, lay the chicken pieces on
the grill rack, and spread the pieces with some of the
marinade left in the dish. Grill for 10 minutes a side.
Meanwhile, preheat the oven to 180°C/350°F/gas mark 4.

Moisten the breadcrumbs with enough of the marinade
to make a crumby paste. Spoon it over the chicken
pieces. Put the chicken in the oven and bake for 15
minutes, to complete the cooking. Allow to cool. Pack in
a plastic box.

Pungent Shrimp Packets

These shrimp packets are not straight Indian fare, owing more to India's neighbour Burma – with a touch of China about the wrappers! But they marry well with the more traditional Indian flavours.

Serves 6

675 g (1½ lb) cooked
   shrimps, shelled
2×175 g (6 oz) cans of
   water chestnuts,
   drained and chopped
A bunch of spring onions,
   chopped
4 tablespoons chopped
   coriander
12 egg roll or large won
   ton wrappers
(available from Oriental
   supermarkets)
2 egg whites, beaten
About 3.5 litres (6 pints)
   water
Oil

For the sauce
3 fresh red chillies
4 cloves of garlic
2 tablespoons sugar
4 to 5 tablespoons rice
   vinegar
Salt

In a bowl, mix together the shrimps, water chestnuts, spring onions and coriander. Put out the wrappers, and place 3 to 4 tablespoons of the mixture in the middle of each. Brush the edges with the beaten egg white, then fold over to make a triangle, pressing the opposite corners together, and securing as firmly as possible.

In a large saucepan, bring the water to the boil. Add a couple of drops of oil. Put in the shrimp packets 2 at a time, and cook for 3 to 4 minutes until the packets are cooked through, but still firm to the bite. Then remove with a slotted spoon to a bowl of iced water, and leave until cooled. Repeat this procedure with all 12 packets. When they are cool, drain.

Meanwhile make the dipping sauce. Pound the chillies and garlic together in a bowl, or blend in a blender or food processor. Add the sugar, vinegar and salt, and combine thoroughly. Pour the sauce into a small covered bowl or box and allow to rest for several hours to give the flavours time to amalgamate.

Pack the shrimp packets into a plastic box. Serve 2 per person, and pass the dipping sauce. It is very sharp and spicy, and only a little need be taken on to each packet.

Golden Sunset Clementines

Makes 5 large jars

1.75 kg (4 lb) clementines
900 ml (1½ pints) water
2 lemons, strained juice
   and pared rind

450 g (1 lb) white sugar
150 ml (¼ pint) brandy
   or Cointreau

Use a saucepan, at least 25 cm (10 in) in diameter, with a steamer. Put the clementines in the basket, and the water in the saucepan. Cover and steam for 15 minutes.

Meanwhile wash thoroughly 5×500 ml (17 fl oz) preserving jars, each holding about 8 fruit. Put the jars, still wet, in a hot oven, leaving their lids open and their rubber seals off. Heat until very hot – about 15 minutes.

Take the basket of clementines from over the water. Pour the water, now enriched with the clementine juice, into a smaller saucepan. Return the clementines to the larger saucepan; cover to keep warm.

Add the lemon juice and rind to the smaller saucepan, and boil for about 2 minutes; then add the sugar slowly, stirring. When the sugar has dissolved bring the liquid back to the boil and keep it on a low boil for about 5 minutes, until it becomes syrupy.

Remove the jars from the oven, and, using a couple of metal skewers, spear the clementines and place them neatly in the jars. Pour over the syrup, making sure to cover the fruit completely. Add about 2 tablespoons of brandy or Cointreau to each jar, then seal. The preserved clementines will keep indefinitely. Take them to the picnic in their jars, and serve them accompanied by bowls of thick cream.

Ayran

Serves 6

150 ml (½ pint) water,
   frozen

250 ml (8 fl oz) thick
   plain yogurt
Pinch of salt

Put the frozen water in a plastic bag and hit with a wooden mallet to crush. Continue until the ice is in small pieces. In a bowl, stir the yogurt into the crushed ice and salt lightly. Decant into a vacuum flask.

A Tempting Feast

*Milton's Satan tempts Christ in the wilderness
with an array of rich foods suitable for
the grandest outdoor meal.*

Our saviour lifting up his eyes beheld
In ample space under the broadest shade
A table richly spread, in regal mode,
With dishes piled, and meats of noblest sort
And savour, beasts of chase, or fowl of game,
In pastry built, or from the spit, or boiled,
Gris-amber-steamed; all fish from sea or shore
Freshet, or purling brook, of shell or fin,
And exquisitest name, for which was drained
Pontus and Lucrine bay, and Afric coast.
Alas how simple, to these cates compared,
Was that crude apple that diverted Eve!
And at a stately sideboard by the wine
That fragrant smell diffused, in order stood
Tall stripling youths rich clad, of fairer hue
Than Ganymede or Hylas; distant more

Under the trees now tripped, now solemn stood
Nymphs of Diana's train, and Naiades
With fruits and flowers from Amalthea's horn,
And ladies of the Hesperides, that seemed
Fairer than feigned of old, or fabled since
Of fairy damsels met in forest wide,
By knights of Logres, or of Lyoness,
Lancelot or Pelleas, or Pellenore,
And all the while harmonious airs were heard,
Of chiming strings, or charming pipes and winds
Of gentlest gale Arabian odours fanned
From their soft wings, and Flora's earliest smells.
Such was the splendour, and the tempter now
His invitation earnestly renewed.
   What doubts the Son of God to sit and eat?

JOHN MILTON *Paradise Regained* 1671

A Tempting Feast

This Mediterranean-style picnic makes a very tempting feast.
Tyropitta, a mouth-watering savoury cheese pie from Greece,
is particularly irresistible.

Cucumber Ribbons with Tomato and Coriander Dressing

Serves 6 to 8

2 large cucumbers, halved
 and seeded
1 tablespoon salt
450 g (1 lb) ripe tomatoes,
 peeled, seeded, and
 chopped
6 spring onions, trimmed
 and thinly sliced
1 clove of garlic,
 blanched, drained,
 peeled and crushed

A handful of fresh
 coriander, trimmed,
 stalks removed, and
 finely chopped
1 tablespoon red wine
 vinegar
A dash of sugar
2 tablespoons olive oil

With a vegetable peeler or a sharp knife, cut the cucumbers down their length into thin ribbons, running along the side of the cucumber so that the ribbons incorporate an edging of green skin. (Alternatively, use the julienne fixture of a food processor, pressing down hard on the cucumber to produce thinner ribbons.) Place the ribbons in a large bowl with the salt, toss and leave to stand for 15 minutes.

In another bowl, mix together the tomatoes, spring onions, garlic, coriander, red wine vinegar, sugar and oil, mashing and beating to combine all the ingredients into a lumpy dressing.

Drain the ribbons thoroughly and pat them dry. Pack them in a plastic box, and the dressing in a small covered pot or bowl. Toss together at the last minute before serving.

Mediterranean Lamb and Aubergine Salad

Serves 6

2 medium aubergines, cut
 into strips
Salt
60 ml (2 fl oz) olive oil
450 g (1 lb) cooked lamb,
 cut into strips
75 g (3 oz) black olives
50 g (2 oz) chopped dates
3 tablespoons pine nuts,
 toasted
2 hearts of lettuce,
 chopped

For the dressing
250 ml (8 fl oz) Greek-
 style yogurt
175 g (6 oz) cottage
 cheese
A large handful of mint
 leaves
1 teaspoon ground cumin
¾ teaspoon cayenne
 pepper
1 teaspoon salt
60 ml (2 fl oz) olive oil
60 ml (2 fl oz) sunflower
 oil
4 tablespoons lemon juice

Put the aubergine strips in a colander and salt them generously; toss to distribute the salt. Let them drain over the sink for 30 minutes or more.

Rinse and dry the aubergine strips and arrange them in a single layer in a baking tray. Drizzle over the olive oil and bake at 200°C/400°F/gas mark 6 for about 25 to 30 minutes, turning the pieces occasionally. Do not let them become mushy. Remove from the oven and cool.

In a large bowl, combine the lamb, olives, dates, pine nuts, chopped lettuce hearts and cooled aubergine strips.

Combine all the ingredients for the dressing in a blender or food processor and blend to a smooth sauce. Pour the dressing over the salad and toss to combine thoroughly. Pack the dressed salad in a plastic box.

Lemon and Lime Chutney

Makes 2 medium jars

450 g (1 lb) lemons, rind, thinly pared, and juice, strained
225 g (½ lb) limes, rind, thinly pared, and juice, strained
40 g (1½ oz) fresh red or green chillies, seeded and trimmed
175 g (6 oz) sultanas
5 onions, peeled and chopped finely
25 g (1 oz) mustard seeds
50 g (2 oz) salt
450 g (1 lb) caster sugar
900 ml (1½ pints) white wine or cider vinegar

Use a food processor to make this chutney. Put the rind from the fruit into the food processor, add the chillies and sultanas, and process until all are finely chopped. Scrape the mixture into a bowl and add the fruit juice, the chopped onions, the mustard seeds, and the salt, sugar and vinegar. Stir the mixture and leave to rest overnight.

The next day, transfer the mixture to a saucepan, set it on a low heat and simmer the chutney, uncovered, for about 2 hours, until it is thick. Bottle in hot sterilized jars. Leave to mature for about 8 weeks before using.

Tyropitta

Serves 6

675 g (1½ lb) fresh spinach
1 large onion, finely chopped
3 tablespoons olive oil
A dash of nutmeg
Salt and pepper
8 sprigs of fresh dill, finely chopped
50 g (2 oz) ricotta or curd cheese
50 g (2 oz) feta cheese, cubed
150 g (5 oz) butter, melted
1 × 400 g (14 oz) packet of prepared phyllo pastry

Wash the fresh spinach thoroughly and remove any large or stringy stalks. Place in a large saucepan, with only the water clinging to the leaves. Cover, and cook over a low heat, taking off the lid to stir and check occasionally, for about 10 minutes, until the spinach is thoroughly wilted. Then leave it to cool.

In a saucepan, sauté the onion in the olive oil until it is transparent. Scrape the onion into a bowl. Squeeze the excess moisture from the cooked spinach, chop it, and add it to the bowl with the onion. Season with nutmeg and salt and pepper to taste. Stir and mash in the dill, the ricotta or curd cheese, and the feta. Combine as thoroughly as possible.

Preheat the oven to 200°C/400°F/gas mark 5. Butter a large tin (about 25 × 20 cm/10 × 8 in), with a shallow rim. Lay about five sheets of phyllo pastry in it, one over the other, brushing each layer with melted butter. Let the edges of the pastry hang out over the tin. Spoon in the spinach and cheese filling, then repeat the layers and the buttering. Fold over all the overhanging edges of phyllo pastry towards the middle of the pie, still buttering between layers. Finally, sprinkle a little water on the top, and cut the pie into smallish squares or diamonds. Bake for about 40 minutes, or until golden. The *tyropitta* can be transported and served still slightly warm, or allowed to cool to room temperature.

Peach Streusel

Serves 6 to 8

50 g (2 oz) cornflour
175 g (6 oz) plain white flour
2 teaspoons baking powder
A large pinch of salt
100 g (4 oz) soft brown sugar
100 g (4 oz) unsalted butter
1 egg
125 ml (4 fl oz) milk
4 peaches, peeled and quartered

For the streusel
50 g (2 oz) plain white flour
50 g (2 oz) Muscovado sugar
1 tablespoon ground cinnamon
½ teaspoon allspice
50 g (2 oz) unsalted butter

Preheat the oven to 190°C/375°F/gas mark 5. In a large bowl, mix together the cornflour, plain flour, baking powder, salt, and brown sugar. Rub in the butter, then beat in the egg and the milk; stir till fully combined.

Pour the dough into a 23 cm (9 in) cake tin, and top with the peach quarters. Combine the flour, sugar and spices for the streusel in another bowl and rub in the butter till the mixture has the consistency of breadcrumbs. Scatter over the peaches.

Put the cake in the oven and bake for 45 minutes. Let it cool before turning it out. Keep in an airtight tin.

Heavenly Picnics

*Not everyone can feast, like Dorothy Wordsworth,
in the company of poets.
But every picnic holds, at least in anticipation,
the promise of perfection.*

We came down and rested upon a moss covered Rock, rising out of the bed of the River. There we lay, ate our dinner and stayed there till about 4 o'clock or later. Wm and C. repeated and read verses. I drank a little Brandy and water and was in Heaven.

DOROTHY WORDSWORTH *The Grasmere Journal* 4.5.1802

Sebastian entered – dove-grey flannel, white *crêpe de Chine*, a Charvet tie , my tie as it happened, a pattern of postage stamps – 'Charles – . . . the whole of Oxford has become *most* peculiar suddenly. Last night it was pullulating with women. You're to come away at once, out of danger. I've got a motor-car and a basket of strawberries and a bottle of Château Peyraguey – which isn't a wine you've ever tasted, so don't pretend. It's heaven with strawberries.'

. . . On a sheep-cropped knoll under a clump of elms we ate the strawberries and drank the wine – as Sebastian promised, they were delicious together – and we lit fat, Turkish cigarettes and lay on our backs, Sebastian's eyes on the leaves above him, mine on his profile, while the blue-grey smoke rose, untroubled by any wind, to the blue-green shadows of foliage, and the sweet scent of the tobacco merged with the sweet summer scents around us and the fumes of the sweet, golden wine seemed to lift us a finger's breadth above the turf and hold us suspended.

'Just the place to bury a crock of gold,' said Sebastian. 'I should like to bury something precious in every place where I've been happy and then, when I was old and ugly and miserable, I could come back and dig it up and remember.'

EVELYN WAUGH *Brideshead Revisited* 1945

Heavenly Picnics

Redolent with the flavours of Austria and Italy, lightened with lovely, golden, oh-so-English Pimm's, this is indeed a banquet for romantics. If you wish to make the first course more substantial, serve a small smoked trout to each picnicker. Its delicate smokiness will be a subtle counterpoint to the spicy-sour cheese.

Spiced Potted Cheese

Serves 4 to 6

150 g (5 oz) cream cheese
100 g (4 oz) unsalted butter
1 sour gherkin, finely chopped
1 tablespoon anchovy paste
1 tablespoon capers, chopped
3 spring onions, finely chopped
A dash of cayenne pepper
1 teaspoon Hungarian sweet paprika

Mash the cream cheese with the butter until they are well combined. Add the remaining ingredients, and mash, fold and stir until all is amalgamated. Pack into an earthenware pot; serve with thinly sliced pumpernickel or rye bread.

Cold Veal with Tuna Mayonnaise

Serves 6

1.5 kg (3 lb) boned and rolled veal roast
1 large carrot, peeled and chopped
2 stalks of celery, chopped
1 glass of white wine

For the sauce
2 egg yolks
1 teaspoon Dijon mustard
Lemon juice
200 ml (7 fl oz) olive oil and sunflower oil, mixed
50 g (2 oz) tuna in oil, drained
Salt and pepper

Preheat the oven to 180°C/350°F/gas mark 4. Place the veal in a roasting tin with the carrot and the celery, and pour over the wine. Cover the tin, put it in the oven and cook for about 2 hours. Remove the lid and allow the roast to cook uncovered for another 30 minutes. Take from the oven and leave to cool.

To make the sauce, beat the egg yolks well, then stir in the mustard and a squeeze or two of lemon juice. Pour in the oil in a thin stream, beating vigorously all the time. Continue until the ingredients are emulsified into mayonnaise. In another bowl, pour.d the tuna to a purée. Gently fold this into the mayonnaise, season to taste, cover and chill.

Cut the cold veal into thin slices. Pack it into a large plastic box, pouring the tuna sauce in between and over the slices. Chill at least overnight to allow the flavours to amalgamate and mellow.

Almond-Sherry Pilaff

Serves 6

100 g (4 oz) angel's hair noodles, broken into very small pieces
50 g (2 oz) butter
225 g (8 oz) long-grain rice
300 ml (½ pint) chicken broth

175 ml (6 fl oz) dry sherry
1 tablespoon chopped tarragon
75 g (3 oz) blanched slivered almonds, toasted
3 lemons

Place the noodles in a frying pan and set it over medium heat. Stir for about 3 minutes, until they are golden-brown. Remove from the heat, and reserve.

Melt the butter, stir in the rice, and heat until the rice is opaque and just toasted, about 3 to 4 minutes. Add the chicken broth, the noodles and the sherry, and stir in the tarragon. Bring to the boil, cover and simmer for about 25 minutes, or until the rice is tender. Remove from the heat and stir in the almonds. Spoon into a plastic box and chill in the fridge till you are ready to leave for the picnic. Take the lemons in a separate bag. Cut them in half, and give each of your guests half a lemon to squeeze over the pilaff.

Pimm's on Ice

Serves 6

1 bottle of Pimm's No. 1
⅓ bottle of gin
2 bottles of ginger ale
225 g (8 oz) strawberries, washed and hulled

2 oranges, peeled and finely sliced in rounds
½ cucumber, finely sliced
Several sprigs of mint
Several sprigs of borage (optional)

Keep the bottles of Pimm's, gin and ginger ale well chilled until just before departure. Then either pack in an insulated box or bag, or wrap in tea towels which have also been kept in the fridge. Bring a large, attractive glass pitcher and glasses with you.

Pack the prepared strawberries, oranges and cucumber in a plastic box. Wrap the mint and borage sprigs in damp tea towels. Fill a large vacuum flask with crushed ice.

To serve, mix the Pimm's, the gin, and the ginger ale in the pitcher. Add some strawberries, orange slices and cucumber slices to the pitcher and put some in each glass. Spoon some of the crushed ice into each glass. Pour over the Pimm's mix, and add sprigs of mint and borage, if available. Cheers!

Picnic Essentials

It is very important to remember to pack the corkscrew, though; and the tin-opener, as George, Harris and J. discovered.

It cast a gloom over the boat, there being no mustard. We ate our beef in silence. . . . We brightened up a bit however, over the apple-tart, and when George drew out a tin of pineapple from the bottom of the hamper, and rolled it into the middle of the boat, we felt life was worth living after all.

We are very fond of pineapple, all three of us. We looked at the picture on the tin; we thought of the juice. We smiled at one another, and Harris got a spoon ready.

Then we looked for the knife to open the tin with. We turned out everything in the hamper. We turned out the bags. We pulled up the boards at the bottom of the boat. We took everything out on to the bank and shook it. There was no tin-opener to be found.

Then Harris tried to open the tin with a pocket-knife, and broke the knife and cut himself badly; and George tried a pair of scissors, and the scissors flew up, and nearly put his eye out. . . .

Then we all got mad. We took that tin out on the bank, and Harris went up into a field and got a big sharp stone, and I went back into the boat and brought out the mast, and George held the tin and Harris held the sharp end of his stone against the top of it, and I took the mast and poised it high up in the air, and gathered up all my strength and brought it down.

It was George's straw hat that saved his life that day. He keeps that hat now (what is left of it), and, of a winter's evening, when the pipes are lit and the boys are telling stretchers about the dangers they have passed through, George brings it down and shows it round, and the stirring tale is told anew, with fresh exaggerations every time.

Harris got off with merely a flesh wound.

JEROME K. JEROME *Three Men in a Boat* 1889

Picnic Essentials

There are some curmudgeonly sorts who don't like picnics. They inveigh against sand in their sandwiches and ants in less conspicuous places. But they are exceptions: the unhappy victims of a deprived, picnic-less childhood, perhaps. Now they have grown too old and sensible to submit themselves to the *laissez-faire* attitude that the perfect picnic demands. Unhappy souls! Let us raise a glass of elderflower champagne (checking first, of course, for stray ants) and drink to their recovery.

That is not to say that picnics need no organizer – that is not at all the case. Some hardy person *must* assume command: make sure that the provisions are prepared, the armaments packed, the bivouac reconnoitred and the plan of action agreed. The last two may be left to a trusted lieutenant – often the driver – but the captain must take responsibility for the first two. Picnic by committee is hardly ever successful: the corkscrew is bound to be forgotten, and both the first and the main course will inevitably turn out to have a rich mayonnaise dressing, or garlic, or both. But the commander must be someone who loves his assignment, the *gourmand* of the crew. Otherwise she (or he) can expect a mutiny – or at least a grumble – when the famished troops set to. An army marches on its stomach.

The commander must also list the non-edible essentials to take on the picnic, and either assemble them her/himself, or delegate the list to someone who shares a respect for planning. Some people love picnics, but assume that they just happen. Do not on any account assign to one of these the assembling of the *mise en scène*. The bonds of friendship should strengthen across the picnic blanket, not be severed for want of a knife!

Some alfresco meals require more than others, but there are certain basics that are elementary to all. A good corkscrew or bottle opener leads the list, followed closely by a sharp knife, even if all the food has been apportioned beforehand. Someone will certainly want half of something. And though some informal picnics, thoughtfully planned to consist entirely of finger food, can do very well without individual knives, forks and spoons, it generally pays to have the odd spoon and fork somewhere in your basket, just in case. Do make sure that there are plates and glasses or cups for everyone in the party: for some reason glasses easily get overlooked, and swigging from the bottle does lower the tone.

Paper napkins should be plentiful – thrills and spills abound when the food is balanced on laps, or on an overloaded table. These napkins are useful, too, for wiping dirty plates and cups before repacking. A damp cloth carried in a plastic bag is bound to come in handy. And a bag for rubbish is a good idea as well. If you are away from it all, including refuse bins, you will want to leave the spot just as unspoiled for the next arrivals.

Depending on the picnic, provisions may be transported in anything from a back pack to a deep wicker picnic hamper. But whatever you use, you will want to organize your food and equipment so that it is easy to carry. Light, unbreakable plastic is a great boon to picnickers. For informal picnics, you can use plastic cups, plates and cutlery. Even if you are intending to furnish your picnic table with porcelain, crystal and silver, you will probably find it very useful to be able to pack some of your food in plastic bags and boxes. And plastic film and aluminium foil are both invaluable for wrapping food, and for covering bowls and boxes.

Vacuum flasks, for carrying hot or cold drinks or soups, have been picnic essentials for a long time. If you are an enthusiastic picnicker, you will also probably find it worth investing in an insulated bag or box for keeping food and drinks cold. However, if you don't have the space or the carrying power for all the refinements, put a few tea towels in the fridge for a couple of hours, and use them to wrap chilled bottles or tins. They will stay cold for a surprisingly long time.

Put a little planning into the packing of your basket, bag or box. It really does make things easier when you reach your picnic spot if you have packed in sequence, from the bottom up – with napkins, plates, cups and cutlery at the top, the first course immediately underneath, and so on down the basket.

At all but the most informal picnics, you will need something to eat off: a collapsible table and light folding garden chairs or stools; or a capacious rug or blanket. If you are using a rug, it is a good idea to take along a groundsheet as well. In some places – often the best picnic spots – the ground never seems to dry out.

Finally, back to the food. If the picnic includes guests whose tastes you do not know, and especially if there are going to be children, it is sensible to hedge your bets by packing additional titbits that are generally popular. These might include tomatoes, celery and carrot sticks, hard-boiled eggs, cheese and biscuits, and fruit.

Then, after all your planning, you too can sit back and enjoy the perfect picnic – in the happy knowledge that it qualifies for the colloquial definition of picnic also included in the dictionary: 'something especially agreeable or easily accomplished'.

Index

List of Plates